ITALIAN CINEMA
1952 - 1965   *Today*

ITALIAN CINEMA
Today

1952 - 1965

Text by *Gian Luigi Rondi*
Foreword by *Bosley Crowther*

HILL AND WANG - NEW YORK

Foreword
by
Bosley Crowther

*I*t is more than a polite professional tribute to the makers of Italian films that so much has been published about them in the United States and other English-speaking countries in recent years. It is a service to the literature of cinema that has been compelled by the extraordinary work — indeed, by the major advances in the development of cinema — that these artists have achieved.

No longer do American film critics hem and haw in acknowledging the fact that the great work in motion pictures has been done outside our country since World War II. We realize beyond any hedging or chauvinistic conceit that this is true. Our Hollywood writers and directors have managed to keep American films comparatively bold and commercially prosperous in these genuinely critical years of excruciating competition with the more elastic television medium. But the real exploration of horizons (beyond the mere mastering of the giant screen), the advancement of motion picture into more complex and disjointed narrative forms, the refinement and use of more subtle and poetic pictorial imagery — in short, the expansion of the medium as a mature communication device — have been done by the foreign film-makers, especially the Italians.

It is not within my province here to tick off what these achievements have been — what, in particular, the Italians have accomplished in the years since the great surge of so-called neorealism subsided to a desultory stream of Cinecittà potboilers, until the flow of creativity again welled from Fellini, Visconti, De Sica, Antonioni and many more. The accomplishments of these artists are the substance of this book.

The works of these men and their impulses are as needful of wise analysis and critical explanation as are the works of Jean-Paul Sartre or Marcel Proust. These are the contemporary authors and poets who are speaking to us of things vital to our generation in the sensory idioms of our age. Their messages and methods are crucial, and they cry to be understood not only by other film-makers (who read much less than they should!), not only by cinema students (who read more than is good for them), but by the incalculable numbers of average movie-goers.

The international scope of motion pictures compels an international literature of films — not alone on the high-brow, cultist levels of a few conspicuous cinema magazines, but on the levels of middle-brow culture and normal intelligence and taste. These are the levels that are needful of more criticism and discussion of films. These are the people in society who have to be inspired and informed.

This volume of exciting discussion of Italian directors who have worked in the fruitful period of 1952-65 is a most valuable contribution to this literature. It provides information and insights that are stimulating and enjoyable. Naturally, being a critic, I do not agree with every estimation that the distinguished Gian Luigi Rondi makes. But being an ardent debater, I delight in matching my judgments with his. And I welcome greatly the abundance of fine photographs of key scenes and characters from films under discussion. They stock the storehouse of my memories!

Introduction
by
Gian Luigi Rondi

Is it possible to write the history of the fifty years from 1895 (the date of Lumière) to 1945 (the end of the Second World War) by searching for the motives, values, aspirations, and interests of the time in the motion pictures made in that period? We would say: definitely not. Perhaps we may find hints of some significance in the American cinema during the First World War and the first postwar period; the French cinema repeats a single cliché around the Second World War, and the German cinema is nothing but absurdity; as for the countries under the rule of dictatorship, any attempt at studying the period gives place to mythical and rhetorical glorification.

What everywhere and above all prevailed was evasion, evasion of circumstances, current events, daily needs, as well as their historical causes. There seemed to be universal agreement all over the world that when a person goes to sit down in a dark hall for the purpose of watching figures in motion on a screen he must not feel that any problem is being presented to him: he already has too many on his mind and has left too many behind at home or in the street. What he asks from the screen is only to be able to believe in the ideal love he has never attained, in the success he has never won, asking at the same time for details (in dreams, of course, not in reality) on how to achieve all these things, delighted to see the hero who wins the woman with a revolver, who forges a position for himself by the strength of his fists, who checkmates the police and the judges, who seems bad, but at the end will turn out good, or at least happy, after all.

And yet, in fifty years the world has changed its appearance once again: Europe and America have faced two wars, almost everywhere in the world a variety of wars has broken out, empires and kingdoms have fallen, labor problems and social problems of a more general nature have come to the fore with a polemical zest at times exceedingly violent, the conflict between man and the machine has taken on occasionally dramatic forms and, in the last analysis, has caused bloody revolutions. The cinema has only to a minimal degree reported a distant echo of these events. And when it has made the attempt, it has either ended up deliberately in farce — note Chaplin's *The Great Dictator* — or has dismally yielded to propagandistic requirements dictated, in general, not by the needs of the public, but by imperious political necessities of the moment — consider the American antiracialist or anti-German films or prowar films in favor of Great Britain; consider, from the opposite side, the German racialist or anti-British films, and so forth.

In Italy, however, suddenly, in the yet uncertain light of a peace hesitantly called an armistice, a series of films appeared which were not born out of propaganda (no authority required them), which were not born out of the wish for evasion (they dealt with the terrible events of those days), and which did not run counter to the wishes of the public (for the public greeted them with enthusiasm and with tears).

What had happened? The Second World War, with its destruction, deaths, and foreign occupations, had jolted the Italians out of the soporific illusions of the rosy, optimistic cinema which for twenty years they had been subjected to by the dictatorship. For twenty years they had been fed on evasions, and the awakening after that, face to face with reality, had been absolutely frightful. Indeed, so immediate and unexpected had been that awakening that there were many things the Italians had not even had time to realize, many things, but above all a problem which had arisen, terrible and unsolved, from all that carnage: the problem of others, the lost and forgotten meaning of the word "neighbor." Who, in the midst of all that bloodshed, had been "my neighbor"? Who, among slayers and slain, persecutors and persecuted, had for an instant remembered the value of that word which, after all, had been pronounced to sound like "brother"? A grave, obscure, insoluble problem — insoluble, above all, in the face of that frightful slaughter which had bathed Italy in blood.

The cinema, however, almost inadvertently, came to outline the solution to such a problem. And as it attempted, confronted, and proposed this solution to those audiences who at last no longer sought evasion (because evasion, to them, now coincided with the discovery of this suspected and feared reality), we see it touching on every contemporary theme, probing to the very depths the roots of the evil from which men had suffered, searching out and discovering the paths of good to which to direct these men. Every contemporary theme: the war, first of all, which was front-page news in those days, and then human sorrow, the tears of men, death; and hatred and the reason for this evil; and the meaning of "neighbor" and the value of the word "others."

And, finally, when these themes had been treated, we see this cinema confronting the daily questions of human life, responding to the vital core of social questions which the cinema, up to that time, had seen only from afar, making a clean break with the uneasy decadence of the postwar period in order to point out other values to live for, other hopes, other needs.

But the vital secret which made this cinema's response worth hearing and which transmitted it to attentive audiences lay in the fact that at the center of its attention, the fulcrum and meeting place of all its concerns, were no longer the fictitious inventions which had allowed the prewar audiences to dream, but contemporary men with real faces and real feelings, caught in the coil of their own real problems, enlightened by real solutions, confronted by real prospects. The novelty in such a cinema, in fact, was its having wanted at all costs to take reality as its subject, not feigned, not reconstituted, not studied just for esthetic effects, but portrayed with faithful humility along the roads and squares and in the houses of Italy.

The history of the Italian cinema from 1945 to 1950 is thus the history of that human and esthetic movement which some theorizers have wished, improperly, to call neorealism and which, in the wider context of the history of the cinema, represents one of the happiest stages in the long journey of the Seventh Art toward the conquest of truth.

If realism had in fact been a way of interpreting reality according to an essentially esthetic need, what was called neorealism obeyed needs which were, on the contrary, less external and more human. Indeed, in those who were its creators it showed itself at once, even in its widely differing forms, to be inspired by a common motive, which, putting to the poets the agonizing problem of communicating with their fellows, drove them, through the very need to be perfectly understood and thus to be able concretely to help, to search for a language as simple and unadorned as possible.

The history of neorealism is thus the history of a dialogue, not, however, of a dialogue embellished with sophisticated intellectualism or guided by those motives of pleasures, amusement, or individual search for perfection and beauty which had directed so much art in the past, but a dialogue in which the interlocutors — poets and auditors — were aware: the first, of the fundamental reality of the moment — sorrow — while the others unconsciously carried it in their hearts, desirous only of help.

The situation in Italy in 1944 was such, moreover, as not to allow the poets more than one theme, sorrow alone, and only one way of expressing it without wounding all those who were its victims: thus they told their fellows what they had suffered and they told it exactly, without superfluous interpretations, not putting themselves egoistically between the sufferers and their sorrow.

Open City by Roberto Rossellini (1945) opens the series: it is the story of a partisan, a priest, and a woman, who, all in equal measure, forsake life in order to defend their faith in freedom and in charity against the Nazi invader. Today, twenty years afterward, the value of *Open City* is even clearer than it seemed in those days, mingled as it was with the violent emotions which immediately took hold of us. Within its story, traces of melodrama are certainly visible, and many of its characters often come near being a little too exclamatory. But in the deliberately bald and unadorned way in which Rossellini described the most dramatic parts of the action, in the harsh reserve with which, in the most significant moments, he restrained himself from seeking after any effect at all are already found the modes and accents of a style which was to become the most significant in the new Italian cinema — a style which sought the truth in order to be able to tell it for the comfort of others, a style which looked upon truth as an esthetic conquest at a time when poetry meant the renunciation of every artifice, the sacrifice of itself, the attainment of the essential.

Somebody said that Rossellini was not exactly aware of the formula created with *Open City*. But if we look at *Paisan*, made immediately afterward, in 1946, we can find in its themes the same accents peculiar to the style of *Open City*, more conscious, perhaps, and even more concretely resolved within the cinematographic medium, in a perfect esthetic unity.

Following the story of Rome, told in *Open City*, *Paisan* is the story of Italy under the Germans, at the dawn of a hard and arduously won liberation: six episodes, each picturing a region of Italy between 1944 and 1945; six episodes and their protagonists, all Italian, almost always meeting death as a result of their encounter with the foreigner — they are bare, arid reporting, apparently distant and impersonal. That objectivity which already in *Open City* bordered on poetry becomes here the motif of tragedy, a tragedy which finds its elements not in the declaimed, the outspoken, the eloquent, but in the lowly, the neglected, the essential, since the topics treated are already in themselves noble and tragic.

It is here that Rossellini's technique, the technique of enclosing the characters for very long sequences in the tireless round of the camera, becomes the most consummate style. His narrative manner can now be clearly defined as that of the eye of a man following events in a public square: the details are reduced to the minimum, the camera is hardly ever taken off the characters, pauses for pondering to let things sink in seem abolished, indulgence in sentimental pleasures is no longer to be found.

The movie camera ranges all over Italy from Sicily to the Po without a stop, always refraining from penetrating into the minds of individuals because the poet today is interested in those things which fill the reports of crime and bloodshed in the daily press: the war, the occupation, the liberation. They are the things that count, things in their wholeness and their crudity, things seen from the outside, so that each person may permeate them with what he had secretly shut up inside himself during those hours when Italy was sown with calvaries and crosses.

Thus, from a form of sad respect for the mind of the audience, a new kind of poetry is born.

Objectivity and detachment, wedded to the singular stylistic boldness of long narrative sequences, with the camera always focused on the principal characters, find a wider expression in *Germany Year Zero* (1947) which Rossellini made directly in Berlin, in the capital from which Italy's sorrow had originated. The theme here was even more difficult: it was not a question of outlining a condition of human misery in order to comfort that misery; it was a question of denouncing the very fall of Europe, showing that the evil had not only descended on our peninsula, but had also wasted all the other nations, in their minds and spirits as well as in their bodies and in their houses. *Germany Year Zero* is total dissolution and, on the part of the poet who feels the sorrow of his times, is the last negative appeal to the good that has been lost.

The speed, the essentiality, the carelessness of certain passages in the film derive from the total absence of formalism with which Rossellini has worked out his stylistic discovery. The camera in the end never abandons the characters and their desolate setting of destroyed houses, and it often holds back from elucidating a problem, from assembling and dissecting an emotion, from deepening an analysis. If this, however, harms the film at some points and weaves into it a suspicion of haste, yet it kindles the essential moments with a high poetic fervor.

In *Stromboli* (1950) the documentary style becomes introspective: the many human faces are replaced by a single one, and of this one he analyses not only the outward movements (justifying them with outward actions), but also and above all the secret motions within the heart, the travail of the conscience. And the film, and the cinematographic language on which the film relies, becomes almost a visual projection of that conscience, interpretations from within of the world around. It is still realism, but reality this time springs from within character.

In this vein, with this style — but made still more ethereal and impalpable by a more delicate breath of poetry — is *The Flowers of St. Francis*: not the life of a saint, but life seen by a saint, earthly reality interpreted in the light of Christian ideas (exactly as, a year later, *Europa '51*).

Vittorio De Sica: 1946 is one of the most important moments in his career, when, with the help of scriptwriter Cesare Zavattini (help which still supports and follows him to whom the Italian cinema owes some of its most fervent pages, above all in the sphere of the grand neorealist style) he made *Shoeshine*, the story of two boys in Italy's postwar period, who, innocent victims of the lack of humaneness among their neighbors, see themselves shut out by human unkindness from every possibility of salvation.

De Sica's style is a different thing from Rossellini's — where we have seen objectivity, detachment, respect for the audience who are offered for meditation real facts to comfort and remind, in the light of a poetry whose basic idea is the exact reproduction of daily reality, we now find a direct and passionate participation in the events denounced. De Sica does not reproduce characters, relying on their inner poetic force, but constructs human figures, dramas, conflicts, with a view to precise, moving, poignant results.

In *Shoeshine*, this manner of his is kept on lines of absolute reserve: the poetry never becomes lyricism and the narrative rhythm never indulges in sentiment; rather, it skims over every detail, every psychological nuance, every fact, even the external ones of the setting, only considering the precise esthetic and polemical aims desired to be reached. De Sica's partiality toward his characters and the personal preciosity of his language preserve a harmony here which never gives rise to sentimentality or jarring notes.

Later (*The Bicycle Thief, Miracle in Milan*), De Sica also entered a certain contentious current which filmed some of the most burning themes of the historical period in which neorealism was born: he expressed them, however, with a whole battery, romantic and precious, of pictorial aims which — if we except, perhaps, the dramatic, almost horrifying tone of *Shoeshine* — even came near delight in form. But this delight, let it be clear, was not De Sica's only contribution as director to the films written for him by Cesare Zavattini, for, indeed, to raise again and in a certain sense settle in the director's favor the debated question of the real author of the film, it was just where the films breathed a definite poetic atmosphere that De Sica's personality and his most authentic influence as an expert creator were most evident. A very clear example is *The Bicycle Thief*, where, as soon as the two protagonists, father and son, are left alone in the town which empties around them and the director pushes them into the closed, painful circle of their destiny of loneliness, suddenly the grand climate of modern tragedy is liberated, with its search for the human element in the character and the sympathetic element in his drama, attempted with firm inspiration and translated materially, visually, pictorially onto the screen with a precision perfectly consistent with the desolation to be evoked.

But perhaps on the plane of this human solitude, which becomes poetry and which the cinema presents to us with a language that seems to spring precisely from this troubled solitude, one of Luchino Visconti's first films, *The Earth Trembles*, has even more to recommend it. Although it has undergone various alterations and can no longer be appraised in its original version, which won a prize at the 1948 Venice Festival, *The Earth Trembles* remains a film of emphatic poetic interest and noble stylistic results.

There is a large measure of neorealism in Visconti, even though he is already (1947-48) abandoning its incidental themes to hazard the universal ones: man's work, his solitude, his struggle to live, his life in the midst of others, love, home, family — the universal themes which had been suggested to Visconti, from a distance, by one of the soundest texts of the old literary realism, Giovanni Verga's *I Malavoglia (The House by the Medlar Tree)*.

The Earth Trembles probes the characters and expresses their human moment with the same clarity with which this moment takes place within them. Its language may be too calligraphic, it may show the effects of pictorial lessons that are often foreign to the setting being represented, and its rhythm may here and there seem too slow, for it is belligerently faithful to that actual tempo which the cinema, on becoming an art, had replaced with an imaginary tempo. But even in this film, we soon discover a definite poetic justification (the same languor and the same outward immobility of the Sicilian people, in contrast with the dynamism of their psychological processes), and so the film in the end commands respect with a solemnity and nimbleness decidedly out of the ordinary.

Yet, if Rossellini was above all the revolutionary innovator who founded a new language in the cinema, with new themes, other creators too, besides De Sica and Visconti, renewed their style about this same time, dealing, especially at the beginning, with almost the same subjects, gripped with near unanimity by the importance of the problems of the hour.

Alessandro Blasetti, who in the prewar Italian cinema had been among the first, if not actually the first, to discover new paths in the search for reality (from *Sole* to *1860* to *Four Steps in the Cloud*), confirmed these discoveries of his, in the light of the renewed stylistic and human concerns, in *Un giorno nella vita*, which, with realism excellently wedded to polemical passion, almost laid the foundations of a new form of drama: in the sphere of a human concern which, although with variations, Blasetti was not to abandon even in films set in periods a long way from our own (*Fabiola*).

So, too, Alberto Lattuada, who graduated from the harsh reporting of *Without Pity* to the flowing choral rhythm of *The Mill on the Po*, one of the happiest points of encounter between realism and literature. So, too, Giuseppe De Santis, who, although indulging in imagism, was often successful in not letting it get the upper hand over that realist lesson which, right from the beginning, had made a profound impression on him (*Tragic Hunt, Bitter Rice*). So, too, Pietro Germi, who, early laying aside detailed reporting (*Gioventù perduta*), confronted terse pages of Italian life (*In nome della legge, Il cammino della speranza*), with a precise sense of reality never divorced from an increasingly thorough attention to the individual considered in the context of the society which produces him.

Thus discovery of reality as it comes into being, careful and often deliberately impersonal analysis of man and his problems, the study of history while it is still news and of news at the moment in which it is becoming poetry — this was neorealism, one of the most vital pages in the history of the Italian cinema, but also in the history of our times, and more than this, one of the pages without which it would be impossible to explain the social, political, and moral history of Italy and, indeed, of Europe, from the end of the Second World War to the beginning of the second half of the twentieth century, five years which for our generation have meant almost more than half a century.

Michelangelo Antonioni

Alessandro Blasetti

Mauro Bolognini

Renato Castellani

Luigi Comencini

Giuseppe De Santis

Vittorio De Sica

Luciano Emmer

Federico Fellini

Pietro Germi

Alberto Lattuada

Carlo Lizzani

Mario Monicelli

Antonio Pietrangeli

Gianni Puccini

Dino Risi

Francesco Rosi

Roberto Rossellini

Franco Rossi

Luchino Visconti

Luigi Zampa

Valerio Zurlini

MICHELANGELO ANTONIONI
Born in Ferrara on September 29, 1912.

Principal films:

Cronaca di un amore; La signora senza camelie; Amore in città (an episode); I vinti; Le amiche; Il grido; L'avventura; La notte; L'eclisse; Deserto rosso; I tre volti (an episode).

In 1955 Michelangelo Antonioni, who was to become one of the most significant creators of the Italian cinema (a creator with thoughtful care and style), presented *Le amiche* at the Venice Festival, a film in which the critics, although with some reservations, recognized an unusual force of language and an austere and authentic narrative style.

Taken one by one, the states of mind of the characters and the inner logic of their attitudes are generally brought out with strict economy. Considered as an ensemble, however, the adventures of the four protagonists in the story — drawn rather freely from *Tra donne sole (Lonely Women)*, included in the volume *La bella estate (The Lovely Summer)* by Cesare Pavese — do not balance each other completely; their alternation is often a little fragmentary, when it does not become downright episodic; and the world in which they live is not always seen with a really critical eye.

The stylistic promise of the film, however, is beyond dispute, as is its steadfast dramatic ambition — all gifts already foreshadowing the development of a creator more and more attentive and aware.

Two years later, *Il grido*. The protagonist is a man who for some time has been living with a woman by whom he has had a daughter. They cannot get married because the woman has a husband who left her many years before. One day, however, the news comes that this husband is dead. Now everything could be put right, but the woman has another lover; she no longer loves the first and, although she had lied up to that moment, she doesn't have the courage, now, to lie when faced with marriage. So she tells everything.

The man is thunderstruck, abruptly loses every reason for existing, and runs away with his daughter through villages and towns along the river — we are on the Po, in one of those regions smothered with fog in winter and always under the threat of floods in autumn. In his wanderings he meets other women: in each one he looks for her, the woman who betrayed him, and each one, therefore, sooner or later disappoints him. Finally, we see him back in his own town, carried there by an absurd hope. But it is the last: his mistress is married

and even has another child. And then he kills himself.

A modern tragedy of loneliness, then, and at the same time an attempt to bring love back among the dramatic (and no longer romantic) subjects of contemporary reality.

However, Antonioni has expressed here those poetical themes which were later to become fundamental for him through the frame and setting, rather than through the psychological pattern and dramatic evolution of the characters. Thus the most vital and poetic passages in the film are those in which the protagonist's heavy weariness of life rises out of those gloomy river views, that snow, that mud, those desolate grey fields; or when it reappears in other forms, in secondary figures met by chance in peripheral situations, in men and women seen almost fleetingly, but all more or less tortured by the same oppressive loneliness, the same sickly mistrust: the prostitute in the hut on the river, for example, the half-easeful, half-discontented life in the house by the gasoline pump (the never-satisfied daughter, the mistreated old father — a singular figure, livelier perhaps than most of the other characters), the little girl the father trails about with him for a while, her games, her poetically childish words, her eyes that see more than they say.

In contrast, in the principal figures, the drama loses something of its precision, except that, where scenes and attitudes allow the direction to give us their poetic state of mind, we have again the exact, very intense emotion (even though reserved and bashful) which the creator wished to suggest. And with a language of such rough and miserly nakedness as to recall the most important examples of early realism in its complete formal perfection: a language which is, and always wishes to be, "painting," but painting modeled only on the most economical drawing, the purest and barest pictorial inspiration.

And now *L'avventura*. The story, this time, is apparently rather simple: it begins with a trip on a yacht, in the frivolous society atmosphere of a world which seems concerned only with enjoying itself. Among the passengers there are two girls: one of them is there

STATEN ISLAND INSTITUTE OF ARTS AND SCIENCES

Staten Island Museum · High Rock Park Conservation Center · William T. Davis Wildlife Refuge

FILM SERIES '89
MICHELANGELO ANTONIONI

JANUARY

8 Sunday, 1:30 pm
Nettezza Urbana, 1948, 9 minutes
L'Avventura, 1960, 145 minutes

15 Sunday, 1:30 pm
La Notte, 1961, 122 minutes, with commentator Bruce Elder

22 Sunday, 1:30 pm
L'Eclisse, 1962, 124 minutes, with commentator P. Adams Sitney

29 Sunday, 1:30 pm
Cronaca di un Amore, 1950, 96 minutes
Tentato Suicidio, 1953, 20 minutes

FEBRUARY

5 Sunday, 1:30 pm
La Signora Senza Camelie, 1953, 105 minutes

12 Sunday, 1:30 pm
Nettezza Urbana, 1948, 9 minutes. *Deserto Rosso*, 1964, 116 minutes, with commentator Giuliana Bruno

16 Thursday, 7:00 pm
[This program at Anthology Film Archives in Manhattan, at 32-34 Second Avenue.]
Gente Del Po, 1947, 10 minutes

L'Amorosa Menzogna, 1949, 10 minutes

Superstizione, 1949, 9 minutes

Le Amiche, 1955, 104 minutes

19 Sunday, 1:30 pm
Blow Up, 1966, 111 minutes

26 Sunday, 1:30 pm
Zabriskie Point, 1970, 110 minutes, with commentator Robert Haller

MARCH

5 Sunday, 1:30 pm
To be announced.

All films at the Museum of the Staten Island Institute unless otherwise noted. These screenings and the gallery exhibition are supported by the New York State Council on the Arts, Film/Video Arts, the Department of Cultural Affairs of the City of New York, the Italian Cultural Institute, and Island Cinema Resources of Staten Island. We are also indebted to the Cineteca Nazionale in Rome, the Museum of Modern Art in New York, and Pacific Film Archives in Berkely for the loan of films, photographs, and services for these projects.

The Staten Island Institute of Arts and Sciences is Staten Island's oldest cultural institution and administers the Staten Island Museum, the Library and Archives, High Rock Park Conservation Center, the William T. Davis Wildlife Refuge, Evergreen Park, and Reeds Basket Willow Swamp. The Institute is supported in part by the City of New York through an annual appropriation from the Department of Cultural Affairs. □

MICHELANGELO ANTONIONI:
THE ENCHANTED MOUNTAINS

Michelangelo Antonioni has been making paintings—abstract and representational—for at least as long as he has been making films. But because he has never allowed them to be seen by the public, or even by many friends, the very existence of this work by one of our greatest film-makers has been unknown. This exhibition, *The Enchanted Mountains*, is the first American show of Antonioni's paintings. The origin of *The Enchanted Mountains* was a series of color tests Antonioni made before shooting began on his first color film, *The Red Desert (Deserto Rosso)* in 1964. By mixing tempera and oil paints on different paper surfaces, Antonioni made the colors that were used in the film, including the painting of whole streets and trees. Six years then passed before he returned to this particular medium (during this time he made both *Blow Up*, 1965, and *Zabriskie Point*, 1970).Starting in the early 1970s, and continuing up through 1985, Antonioni made more than 180 prints in *The Enchanted Mountains* series. In each case he mixed colors on several different paper surfaces, but also had these works collaged, photographed, enlarged and color filtered. The product of this process, which Antonioni performs directly, or supervises in the darkroom, is this photographic series.In 1980 some friends urged him to show the prints to the public, but Antonioni demurred. For two more years he refused these requests, but finally agreed in 1983; their first public exposure came at the Galleria Nazionale d'Arte Moderna from 8 October to 27 November, in conjunction with the Venice Film Festival's award to Antonioni of its Golden Lion for his career in film. Antonioni chose not to comment on the meaning of these works in the catalog for that 1983 show in Rome, save for the title, "Le montagne incantate." In that catalog he limits himself to some basic notes that the photographic enlargement process, like that in the film *Blow Up*, makes visible details "invisible in the original" collage paintings. However, his title *The Enchanted Mountains* suggests a great deal about the pictures; many can easily be perceived as landscapes. But if some are analogous to mountain ranges, others appear to be almost microscopic details of

glacial formations, or aerial perspectives of eroded terrain. These latter readings then prompt us to revise our sense of the "mountain" images. Their depth becomes uncertain, as well as such factors as orientation in space; the juxtaposition of textures and the identification of "horizons" are additional variables. This shifting, this transformation of what we see into what we can not know, contributes to the "enchantment" of the series. The pictures also suggest, in some cases, surrealist frottage, Japanese landscapes, and the luminous paintings of J.M.W. Turner. Of all the comparisons we can seek, the most obvious and most difficult is to Antonioni's films. Visually there are few parallels, but in metaphoric terms the divergent forces of older and more recent moralities, of male disconnection with emotions and honesty, and the female integration of them, are mirrored in these pictures where earth meets air, or less specifically, where one form of matter encounters another.

Robert Haller
Curator of Film, Staten Island
Institute of Arts and Sciences

with her lover, a man still quite young, but in spite of their close relationship, she does not seem to get along with him.

Suddenly this girl disappears. Whether she was drowned, kidnapped, or whether she ran away is not known. Her lover and the others set about a frenzied search for her, but fail to find out anything further about her. During this search, however, the lover and the other girl, united in the same anxiety, end up by falling in love with each other and, in spite of a first attempt at resistance (considering the circumstances), soon yield completely.

But the search continues, and he, though he loves her, finds time to let himself get involved in a dreary transient affair. She is aware of it, and instead of leaving him, she stays. She stays because she knows what feelings are today, because pity in her is stronger even than jealousy, stronger even than love.

To translate such deep, secret anguish into images, Antonioni's style has become even rougher and balder, deliberately ridding itself of the traditional impedimenta of cinematographic narration. (This is the beginning, for example, of those characters of whom we know nothing and who only gradually become clear to us, always indirectly and always within the limits of their feelings, never along the boundaries of their social situation.)

Later on, when the girl disappears (in a primitive, eerie setting of sun-struck Sicilian islands), the atmosphere becomes almost enigmatic, by a singular resemblance recalling Maeterlinck and Kafka, at once striking in its realism and disturbing in its mystery, pregnant with continual allusions. And then the real drama — the drama of the two hearts that seek each other, betray each other, and take each other back, always a little oppressed by the memory of the girl who has disappeared. Here Antonioni has expressed himself almost exclusively by subtle evocations of atmospheres and states of mind, and by sudden psychological intuitions, at the same time managing with polished exactness to keep watch over the surroundings (a Sicily as fresh and lovely as ever), the other characters, and the background situations. He gives us a desolate work, in many places horrifying and in some moving, with a style and technique which this time achieve the most perfect fusion among all the secondary factors too, from the music to the sound and the photography.

In *La notte* we are in the same climate as in *L'avventura*. There is a crisis here too, and here too the crisis concerns the feelings, athough it afterward extends to a whole society. It is suffered by a woman married for years to a man whom she finally ceases to love, since she has seen him gradually falling from the pedestal on which she had placed him, a man tired and disheartened, incapable of arousing real feelings and, without knowing it, incapable of having them himself. When the woman realizes what is happening to her, and her eyes are opened by the death of a friend whom she could have loved and esteemed very differently, she goes off, wandering aimlessly for a day and a long night, in the hope perhaps of finding something firm to hold on to again. In her wandering (which, among its various stops, includes one at a party of rich, rather inane people), at a certain moment the woman finds herself with her husband to whom, in the end, she reveals the discovery she has made, only to receive a reply no more than superficially consoling, yet another proof, in fact, of the

man's emotional poverty, his shallowness, and, ultimately, of his impotence in the face of the crisis which has destroyed him from within.

To tell us about this crisis and, above all, to make it clear to us without ever plainly stating it, Antonioni has tried to make it spring from the description of what the protagonist meets up with in her wanderings, giving her reactions one by one, fitting them in with her surroundings or with the other characters, avoiding the precise delineation of gestures, situations, and states of mind, and leaving us to guess them only through the allusions and references of a language which, while having something in common with the cinema, is almost always derived from literature, and the most inward, the most recondite, the most obscure literature at that.

Consider, for example, the mysterious, always allusive influence the friend's death has on the action, and how it gives particular overtones to the protagonist's first wandering in search of the places where, in far-off days, her love for her husband was born. How full of illusion, afterward, is that walk, how charged with realistic accents, although moving almost in a world of fantasy and unreality, being above all the projection of a feeling, the specter of a memory.

Later on, in its apparent disorder, how clear and stark is that night party in which the chorus of the others assembles around the two protagonists, a chorus perhaps equally despairing and straining after goals it is ignorant of, which it dimly seeks in apathy and doubt.

These pages are " written " with a pen which seems to get clogged in a not very flowing rhythm, but which in reality succeeds in evoking, with rare technique, the most hidden atmospheres, the most impalpable and mysterious climates. It is here, perhaps, that the film reveals its greatest power of suggestion — in its inward character which, making use almost of pantomime, unveils for us the most recondite themes without ever dealing with them directly, letting them be suggested instead by other details, in a sultry atmosphere of things hushed up, expressed always and only from the inside.

The crisis of love, a consequence of the more general crisis undermining mankind in our time and a very clear mirror of the evils that are destroying us, is fundamental for *L'eclisse* too. Here the heroine can no longer love a man to whom she has been tied for years, and she leaves him; she leaves him because she realizes he will never be able to understand what she expects from love, and because she realizes also that she could never make him understand. A few days later she meets a young man who is the opposite of him (and of herself as well) — definite, decided, dynamic, eager for life. He is a stockbroker and the only thing he worships is money. She is aware that he likes her as a lively young man likes a beautiful young woman, and even while sensing that he is so different, she trusts, though with reluctance, to the hope of a new attempt, to the possibility of an encounter in which she might succeed in explaining herself — in explaining, in asking, in having.

But she is too much shut up inside herself to be able to speak, and he is too much the child of his own time to perceive what she is not able to bring to light within herself, in her mind stifled by too much " I don't know, " " I don't understand, " " I don't see. " And since for him love is only sex, that is the only note he sounds with her.

It is a note, however, which is not enough for her

and which he, distracted by the whirlwind of his too active life, must subject to continual variations, to perpetual quick changes: so, following an afternoon of passion, they make an appointment which neither intends to keep, because they both know it is pointless. And everything ends.

The awareness of this pointlessness is the poetic key to the film, as is also the painful sensation of this transformation of men into things, of this subjection of the individual to the overpowering material world which surrounds him on every side, impeding his every gesture, stifling his every word, obscuring his vision. Antonioni has described this transformation in the inner life of three perfectly realized characters in a style which has brilliantly succeeded in matching the significance of the drama, a style which has isolated the characters in the midst of things in order better to show us the influence that things were gradually exercising over them, and which — when he wrote the splendid pages about the Stock Exchange (horrifying X-ray of the myth of gold) or when he put the affair in the ultramodern setting of the EUR in Rome (an architectural anticipation of a future as yet unfulfilled) — has striven to give lyrical expression at every step to the states of mind of the protagonists: their fear of emptiness, their searching, and above all the terrible vanity of this searching. He thus gives life to an action which, notwithstanding the austerity of themes and modes always so congenial to him, is perfectly able to meet the most intelligent requirements of the cinema story — even though deliberately understood as a literary text insofar as psychological developments and accentuation of states of mind are concerned.

Antonioni's *Red Desert*, which won him a Gold Lion at the 1964 Venice Film Festival, is somewhat less elaborate than *L'eclisse* but in many ways equally noteworthy.

Once again Antonioni has given us an instance of the human failure to communicate (foremost among his themes). This time, however, while the failure appears to be a consequence of our modern human condition, Antonioni traces its origin to a specific incident, a trauma, a neurosis in no way linked to our contemporary way of life, our society, or the difficulties of our relationships but, purely and simply, to the state of shock suffered in a car accident.

Are we actually to believe that the modern human predicament Antonioni has portrayed on film has a wholly concrete and accidental cause? If we have all along believed in Antonioni as a poet of the social ills of our time, a mirror of our epoch, one-sided perhaps but always crystal clear, it is difficult indeed to believe in an Antonioni who aspires to be the poet of our mental diseases.

His scenes are oppressed by the somberness of an almost monochromatic winter landscape where the vestiges of a recent snowfall dominate every detail. His pictorial images are first and foremost the reflection of what his characters feel and suffer; they are but the chromatic configuration of a neurosis; the coloration given to objects, people, and the world at large by someone who has suddenly lost every meaningful contact with them. The colors that predominate are therefore drained, "colorless," unreal, white, gray, milky,

smoky — all the subtle gradations of mist. Even when there is bright light to illuminate a scene and reveal objects in their normally varying shades of color, those few dim colors persist — the colors of a rainy morning or a wintry dawn which cast their pall over all of nature. When an occasional colorful detail does stand out to relieve this twilight world (with its whitewashed woods and creamy blades of grass), it bears no resemblance to the colors of the real world but is indeed an abnormal coloration by which the characters convey their feelings and, singling out some particular detail, fixate upon it, exaggerate it, and interpret it.

In partial justification of such a pronounced "departure" it must be said that Antonioni's interest in the symptoms and effects of neurosis, analyzed from the viewpoint of pathology, is not really so far removed from the motives at work in his examination of social and moral estrangement. Upon closer inspection, we may find that the one has been provoked by the other. After so many abstract maladies, perhaps Antonioni felt the need to deal with them more concretely, in the guise of the most commonplace occurrence.

This explanation is confirmed if we examine the means by which Antonioni translates his story onto the screen, employing a technique whose sheer expressiveness does not suffer by comparison with his preceding films. Surpassing in its inventiveness, it is a technique to command our most admiring attention: a new use of color whose effects have never before been achieved on the screen.

Here again, Antonioni's cinematographic language is strictly economical, essential. At the same time, he takes complete liberty with every dramatic convention. Situations, their source and development, never obey the traditional rules of "plot" and "narration" but appear before us in fragments, often without beginning, without resolution. Their scale and narrative weight hold no interest for their creator who looks instead (and exclusively) for the state of mind hidden within the turns and twists of the narrative, revealed in the course of the story. Situations are based not on any logical sequence of events, but arise solely in the characters' psychological evolution and owe their significance to their emotional import rather than any action. The film has action, but it is a secondary element, merely framing the thoughts, desires, and feelings of the characters.

This hierarchy of concerns is realized technically in a sequence of exquisitely balanced, usually static, images (rich in internal rhythm), which are externally sustained in a slow, relaxed breath. The mood thus created perhaps risks sacrificing the typical cadence of cinematographic theatre, but Antonioni substitutes this with a concentration so dramatically and psychologically intense that it captures at least the rapt attention of the provident spectator.

Furthermore, in emphasizing psychological truth over external events — and here we come to what is perhaps the most provocative element in the film — Antonioni chooses his very colors to project his characters' inner feelings, much as Wagner used music to illuminate words. In his subjective use of color he has fulfilled technically and dramatically a vision of aesthetic perfection.

Antonioni's Le Amiche looks like a film still tied to the patterns of the old literary cinema, but in reality it opens the way to a new narrative form, in spite of basic irregularities which prevent it from being perfectly finished.

Michelangelo Antonioni

LE AMICHE

Eleonora Rossi Drago, Gabriele Ferzetti, Franco Fabrizi, Valentina Cortese, Yvonne Furneaux, Ettore Manni (Trionfalcine, 1955).

21

Michelangelo Antonioni

Il grido

Steve Cochran, Alida Valli, Dorian Gray, Lyn Shaw, Gabriella Pallotta, Betsy Blair (S.P.A., 1957).

Il Grido marks Antonioni's first definite success. His culture and his literary inclinations here find a happy meeting point with realistic themes, in the light of psychological complexes. The photography, while always seeking for elaborate pictorial solutions, becomes barer, more immediate.

Michelangelo Antonioni

L'AVVENTURA

Gabriele Ferzetti, Monica Vitti, Lea Massari, Dominique Blanchar, Renzo Ricci (Cino del Duca - Soc. Cin. Lyre, 1959).

L'Avventura opens the great trilogy on the crisis of love, on the romantic, and at the same time very real, shipwreck of every sentiment. Antonioni achieves a poetical atmosphere, rarefied and impalpable, which, notwithstanding its intentional visual concreteness, at times even seems inspired by Kafka's secret hallucinations, by Maeterlinck's fantastic undercurrents.

Michelangelo Antonioni

LA NOTTE

Marcello Mastroianni, Jeanne Moreau, Monica Vitti, Bernhard Vicki, Rosy Mazzacurati, Maria Pia Luzi (Nepi Film - Sofidetip, Silver, 1960).

La Notte probes the crisis more deeply and expresses it with very free narrative rhythms, open to any literary suggestion, deliberately outside the conventional canons of cinematic storytelling, at times along the lines of the " new novel ."

Michelangelo Antonioni

L'ECLISSE - THE ECLIPSE

Monica Vitti, Alain Delon, Francisco Rabal, Lilla Brignone (Interopa Film - Cineriz - Paris Film, 1961).

With The Eclipse, the trilogy on the crisis of the feelings is complete. Incommunicability in love could not have found a more lucid and dramatic narrative expression — in a cinematographic language which seems to repeat and renew the best experiments of abstract painting.

In Red Desert Antonioni again deals with the theme of lack of communication, in a story which unfolds at times with restraint, at times with excitement, according to the state of mind of the characters, which is revealed by a psychological use of color.

Michelangelo Antonioni

DESERTO ROSSO - RED DESERT

Monica Vitti, Richard Harris, Carlo Chionetti, Xenia Valdieri, Aldo Grotti.

ALESSANDRO BLASETTI

Born in Rome on July 3, 1900.

Principal films:

Sole; Nerone; Resurrectio; Terra madre; Palio; 1860; *Vecchia guardia; Aldebaran; Contessa di Parma; Ettore Fieramosca; Retroscena; Un'avventura di Salvator Rosa; La corona di ferro; La cena delle beffe; Quattro passi fra le nuvole; Nessuno torna indietro; Un giorno nella vita; Fabiola; Prima comunione; Altri tempi; Tempi nostri; Peccato che sia una canaglia; Io amo, tu ami...; Le quattro verità (an episode); Liolà; Io, Io e gli altri.*

Alessandro Blasetti, who has given the Italian cinema some of its liveliest works even during that bleak period which is ironically called the "white telephone" age, has in recent years continued to make films. If the moral commitment that had often sustained him in the past is not predominant in these later pictures, the care for style that had enabled Blasetti, even in thorough-going neorealism, to maintain a formal perfection has at least been upheld.

So, after being the colorful inventor of some of the happiest genres in our cinema, now we have him discovering quite an unusual type of cinema story inspired by rather short literary texts, so as to form films consisting of episodes, all based on works of sure taste. *Altri tempi (Times Gone By)* — the first of a series — is based on stories by the best-known Italian writers of the nineteenth and early twentieth centuries and, though obviously lacking an external narrative unity in view of the intentional diversity of themes and subjects, it almost always achieves its own aesthetic unity thanks to the imaginative enthusiasm, the verve, and the fantasy, at times satirically inclined, with which the director has succeeded in guiding and balancing the dance of his characters.

In the same vein is *Tempi nostri (Our Times)*, a second "medley," devoted this time not to the times of our grandparents, but to the present and, for this reason, animated by those polemical intentions which Blasetti always reveals when he deals with contemporary things. The face of our age, he says, is still marked by war; its consequences we can find everywhere, but sorrow, its first consequence, must certainly not lead us to despair, because in each one of us, Blasetti insists, there are still profound reasons for facing life. Let us consider,

then, the protagonist of the first episode (*Mara*, by Pratolini): she is a good country girl who has come to town out of hunger. She has not found an honest job and has begun to walk the streets. But she meets a good man who falls in love with her and will help her to start a new life. And the characters of *Pupo* (freely adapted from a story by Moravia) — are a married couple who, driven by destitution, abandon their child to public charity. But they have hardly committed this act when they both repent of it and rush to put it right. So too in *Casa d'altri (Somebody Else's House)* from a short story by d'Arzo, there is a pitiful old woman who would like to kill herself because she is too poor and weary, whose confidence, instead, is restored when her parish priest succeeds in proving to her, almost in a practical way, that everybody can be useful to others. And so on with the other episodes, always sustained by a hearty optimism.

Certainly the film may seem rather uneven, but some of its sequences breathe a sincere dramatic ardor, and they are the ones which will endure.

Less enduring, however, will be those which rely only on the most playful mirth, on the level of the Italian-style comedy, in *Too Bad She's Bad*, or those complicated by polemical intentions, in *I Love, You Love*, in which Blasetti, returning once more to the film of episodes, is involved in a sort of investigation up and down the world and has not quite achieved those results, even human and social, which he was aiming at.

Nevertheless, his remains a vein still lively and sparkling which, whether he expresses light themes or tackles particularly involved problems, more often than not achieves positive results.

Blasetti's frame is always well composed and harmonious, balanced in its every part, alive to the most searching demands of representationalism, but without ever overwhelming, in its formal perfection, the humanity of the characters or the sincerity of their drama, even when, as in Times Gone By or in Our Times, it draws its inspiration from confessedly literary sources.

Alessandro Blasetti

ALTRI TEMPI - TIMES GONE BY

Andrea Checchi, Alba Arnova, Arnoldo Foà, Folco Lulli, Antonio Centa, Vittorio De Sica, Amedeo Nazzari, Paolo Stoppa, Rina Morelli, Sergio Tofano, Gina Lollobrigida, Virgilio Riento, Aldo Fabrizi, Roldano Lupi, Elisa Cegani, Umberto Melnati (Cines, 1951).

Alessandro Blasetti

TEMPI NOSTRI - OUR TIMES

Vittorio De Sica, Lea Padovani, Marcello Mastroianni, Alba Arnova, Elisa Cegani, Daniele Delorme, Yves Montand, François Perier (Cines - Lux Film - Lux Comp. Cin. De France, 1953).

These sources enable Blasetti to introduce a new formula to the Italian cinema, a composition of short stories perfectly balanced and finished in themselves in spite of the deliberate conciseness of their form.

Alessandro Blasetti

Peccato che sia una canaglia
Too bad she's bad

Vittorio De Sica, Sophia Loren, Marcello Mastroianni (Docum. Film, 1954).

34

Blasetti's cinematographic interests are composite and varied. Always on the lookout for new genres with which to revivify the best currents of the Italian cinema, he goes from light comedy (Too Bad She's Bad) to travel reportage (I Love, You Love) and brief burlesque like the episode of "The Hare and the Tortoise" in Four Truths, always bearing in mind the needs of the spectacle but harmonizing it, more than often not, with respect for serious, committed cinema.

Alessandro Blasetti

Io amo tu ami - I love you love

Nonprofessional actors (Dino De Laurentis Cinemat. S.P.A., 1960).

35

Alessandro Blasetti

LE QUATTRO VERITÀ (La Lepre e la Tartaruga)
FOR TRUTHS (The Hare and the Tortoise)

Monica Vitti, Rossano Brazzi, Sylva
Koscina (Lece Film, 1963).

Alessandro Blasetti

Liolà

Ugo Tognazzi, Giovanna Ralli, Pierre Brasseur, Anouk Aimée (Film Napoleon - Federiz - Cinecittà - France Cinema Production - Francinex, 1964).

MAURO BOLOGNINI

Born in Pistoia on June 28, 1922.

Principal films:

Gli innamorati; Giovani mariti; La notte brava; La giornata balorda; Il Bell'Antonio; La viaccia; Senilità; La corruzione; I tre volti (an episode).

Right from his first appearance in the Italian cinema, Mauro Bolognini revealed a predilection at once pictorial and literary which, while always moving in the sphere of realism and at times even of neorealism, reflected cultivated tendencies, of French origin, of a serious and mature interplay between reality and painting.

He showed us this at once with *Youth in Love*, the story of a love affair set in Trastevere, in which, amid rows, reprisals, love play, misunderstandings, and teasings, while letting the Trastevere surroundings suggest what frankness, vivacity, and roughness could be offered him by realism, he was already revealing literary intentions which, even without being clearly indicated, were almost completely in tune with the world of a Belli or a Goldoni.

Later on, with *Young Husbands*, the same subject is viewed from the angle of a different social class — in *Youth in Love* it was the working class, here it is the provincial middle class. But the atmosphere at once gay and sad remains the same, and already themes and problems are posed which, without exactly developing into social mediations, at any rate seek to solve definite questions of the psychology of modern man and of contemporary customs.

The Night Out, however, is debatable and has, in fact, been debated. Here the young people of Trastevere, considered in a graceful literary key in *Youth in Love*, are now examined in the light of a crude, pitiless neorealism which is certainly not pleasing, and which, to remain on the subject of literature, was suggested to Bolognini by the writings of Pier Paolo Pasolini, all directed to a completely frank inquiry into the life of the Roman slums. Bolognini continues this inquiry, with

equally doubtful results, in *From a Roman Balcony* where, however, as if rebelling against his themes for being too blatantly centered on the crudest realities, he takes pleasure in airing a language increasingly precious and calligraphic, inconsistent with his characters but not with his cultural aspirations.

These aspirations, once the Pasolini literary phase has been left behind, find full and complete development in the films which follow, beginning with that *Bell'Antonio* which Bolognini quarried with painful sensitivity from Vitaliano Brancati's novel of the same name. Here he achieved an almost perfect fusion between the language of literature and that of the cinema, with a style over which he now seemed to have gained an increasingly sure mastery, even though the characters of the novel (who had their own *raison d'être*, especially if viewed a little in an atmosphere of caricature), have become hollow and grotesque, like tragic masks, and have revealed a humanity which, through being utterly exasperated, is frequently nearer exaggeration than it is to a sense of human proportion.

A better film is *The Bad Road*, also drawn from a literary work. Bolognini has directed it with a seriousness, a care for style, and a dramatic rigor which are truly remarkable, measuring out the encounters between the characters with a sure, audacious touch, sustained and guided at every step by a realist inspiration, now harsh, impetuous, wretched, now deliberately turned to nuances of a deeply literary nature. His pictorial predilection gives his language an unaccustomed dignity, a rare, cultured nobility, to which is added the charm of a group of characters all surprised in a *fin de siècle* Florence, recalled with the color and atmosphere of an old print, all speaking the language of the period. Obviously it is a language rich in the witticisms and colorful expressions characteristic not only of the town but also of the country around Florence, yet a language which is still always the "real" Italian, which may be found in everyday speech just as much as in a literary text.

But the film in which Bolognini has achieved the meeting point between cinema and literature in the liveliest way is unquestionably *Senilità* (*When a Man Grows Old*), drawn from Italo Svevo's celebrated novel.

The protagonist is a Trieste intellectual, guileless and unwary, all high-mindedness and youthful innocence (in spite of his forty years). He succumbs to the charms of a beautiful young blonde, full of vitality and warmth, who seems to him at first to be virtuous and modest. He falls deeply in love with her, respects her and worships her with an almost religious devotion, but his poverty, his lack of courage, and the presence in the house of an unmarried sister whom he is obliged to think of, prevent him from speaking of marriage, and eventually lead him to advise the girl to accept any marriage with a man who could give her a home without taking her away from him. When, however, she not only shows herself ready to follow this advice, but actually turns out to be a loose woman, greedy and untruthful, with a past anything but commendable, the intellectual soon falls a prey to a furious jealousy, which, far from lessening when, almost out of contempt, he becomes the girl's lover, rises to such a pitch as to make him, in the end, prefer a final, though heartrending separation.

To put this contrast on the screen was not easy, particularly because of the complexity and apparent contradictions in the protagonist's character, with his irresolution, his false disinterestedness and his genuine weakness, the fruit of credulity and inexperience, almost of humility. Bolognini, however, has confronted the task with a solid cultural background, and with results which, although with some uncertainties, may be considered in large measure successful.

It is true that the principal character is less shy and irresolute than Svevo's and his encounter with the woman, whose character is stronger and more feline than in the novel, shows some obscurities and even certain incongruities accentuated by the shifting of the action from 1898 to 1927, to a period, that is, when the romantic mistake of taking a loose woman to be virtuous is less likely. But even with these changes, the human and moral dimensions of Svevo's work suffer no diminution; rather, the director succeeds in expressing them with austere nobility: in the duet between the two lovers, for example, prepared, developed, and then concluded in the same painful climate of questionings, repressed passions, and pretences which the writer had entrusted to it; in the clever alternation of the minor characters (the sister, in particular, and the sculptor friend); and in the Trieste setting where, in spite of the change of period, he has succeeded in faithfully preserving the desolate, barren, wintry atmosphere which is one of the merits of the novel.

And all is done in a style which, except for a superfluous, completely un-Svevian finale, achieves scenes in which brilliance of composition is happily wedded to the immediacy of a patiently reconstructed reality.

Mauro Bolognini

GIOVANI MARITI - YOUNG HUSBANDS

Isabelle Corey, Antonio Cifariello, Franco Interlenghi, Anna Maria Guarnieri, Raf Mattioli, Rosy Mazzacurati, Gerard Blain, Ennio Girolami, Antonella Lualdi, Sylva Koscina (Nepi Film, 1957).

40

The Night Out represents for Mauro Bolognini a concession to the facile realistic themes of the moment, interpreted in the light of certain writings by Pasolini.

Mauro Bolognini

LA NOTTE BRAVA - THE NIGHT OUT

Rosanna Schiaffino, Elsa Martinelli, Laurent Terzieff, Jean Claude Brialy, Franco Interlenghi, Antonella Lualdi, Anna Maria Ferrero (Ajace Film, 1959).

41

Mauro Bolognini
LA GIORNATA BALORDA
FROM A ROMAN BALCONY

Jean Sorel, Lea Massari, Jeanne Valerie, Rick Bataglia, Paolo Stoppa (Euro International Film - Transcontinental Film, 1960).

IL BELL'ANTONIO - BELL'ANTONIO

Marcello Mastroianni, Claudia Cardinale, Pierre Brasseur, Rina Morelli, Fulvia Mammi, Tomas Milian (Cino Del Duca, Arco Film - Soc. Cin. Lyre, 1960).

The same realism, based on Pasolini, is found in From a Roman Balcony. But Bolognini was to find his real vocation — which is literary in a scholarly way and cinematographic in a highly pictorial way — in Bell'Antonio, with which he began a successful series of films directly inspired by works of definite cultural value.

Pictorial elements, zest in recalling an epoch, psychological accuracy, and, above all, warm perfection of photography are found in The Bad Road, one of Bolognini's films where the novel fits more happily into the scheme of the cinema story.

Mauro Bolognini

LA VIACCIA - THE BAD ROAD

Jean Paul Belmondo, Claudia Cardinale, Pietro Germi, Paul Frankeur, Rina Morelli, Gabriella Pallotta, Romolo Valli, (Arco Film - Titanus - Galatea, 1961).

45

When a Man Grows Old, drawn from Svevo's novel, has been criticized by Svevo admirers for some places where Bolognini has departed from the text he was inspired by; but it is a work of sound dramatic intensity and, in the reconstruction of the place and period in which it is set, distinctly flawless.

Mauro Bolognini

SENILITÀ - WHEN A MAN GROWS OLD

Claudia Cardinale, Anthony Franciosa, Betsy Blair, Philippe Leroy, Stefano Balli (Zebra Flm - Aera Film, 1961).

LA CORRUZIONE - CORRUPTION

Alain Cuny, Rosanna Schiaffino, Jacques Perrin (Arco Film, 1964).

RENATO CASTELLANI

Born in Finale Ligure on September 4, 1913.

Principal films:

Un colpo di pistola; Zazà; La donna della montagna; Mio figlio professore; Sotto il sole di Roma; E' primavera; Due soldi di speranza; Giulietta e Romeo; I sogni nel cassetto; Nella città l'inferno; Il brigante; Mare matto; Controsesso (an episode).

An eclectic creator, combining strong literary inspirations with careful observations of everyday life, Renato Castellani became a triumphant success in the Italian cinema with *Two Pennies' Worth of Hope* (1952), in which he revived the dramatic themes of neorealism with a humorous touch sometimes reminiscent of old Renaissance *novelle*, and sometimes of Basile of the *Cunto delli Cunti,* achieving results of a sparkling freshness in the warm sincerity of a songlike atmosphere.

The same story — the thwarted love of two young people, stifled in the quarrelsome atmosphere of a village feud — was taken up again later by Castellani in a work with grand cultural ambitions. *Romeo and Juliet,* according to the author himself, was intended to be a *Two Pennies' Worth of Hope* in Shakespearean key and, at the same time, the discovery not only of Shakespeare's Italian sources, but also of his secret classical leanings.

Thus, from beginning to end the film unfolds the Shakespearean text before our eyes, always bringing out his innermost logical reasons, his secret motives, and with the point and counterpoint of the narrative developed in a very clear play of situations, each one closely linked to the next, each one arising out of what precedes, each one the cause of what follows. The fiery, colorful Shakespeare, rebel against every rule of drama, wild developer of those canons of the Elizabethan theatre which all added up to freedom of mode and expression, here becomes the confirmed advocate of a meticulous stage alchemy, the convinced supporter of an edifice with fixed, classical lines, where everything finds its place, its function, its consonance, its rule.

But Castellani did not stop here, at this rediscovery of a classical and "Italian" conception of *Romeo and Juliet.* The plan had to be Italian, Italian and classical the narrative conception, Italian also the spirit, the style, the figurative taste: Italian in the way Shakespeare could have pictured them to himself, in the way the *novellieri,* from whom he borrowed his wonderful stories, thought of them. Thus the film offers us a dazzling succession of images of rare beauty, constructed and reconstructed or interpreted in accordance with the most magnificent Renaissance painting, while for the outdoor scenes it depends on Italian cities and fifteenth-century churches in Verona and Siena (the cathedral of Verona, San Zeno Maggiore).

There is not a single moment in which the development of a character or a scene does not recall one of the most celebrated paintings of Piero della Francesca or Pollaiolo, Masaccio, Carpaccio, or Lippi (and here and there reminiscences of Hieronymus Bosch are not lacking). Glorious painting is paraded before our eyes, to become not only the setting, but a living thing, the raw material of a drama of love, aching with suspense and longing, the tense atmosphere of flesh and blood humanity. And when this painting does not inspire an image, it is always its manner which suggests the lines, the composition, and the colors — enchanted, moving colors, which even on the silks, the tapestries, the human faces always have the slightly pale tones of a fresco, its delicate shadows, its soft chiaroscuro, colors which for whole scenes often play on only two tints (yellow ochre and sienna, for example), or on a single tonality suffused with touches of pink and gold (as in the enchanted sequences of the convent at Verona, or the hieratic, near mysterious scenes of the funeral in the church of San Zeno which take on sunset hues, shades of underwater sunshine or ripe ears of corn). And then, of course, the warmer, sharper colors which appear on all the costumes of the characters, at once recalling period portraits, with the difference that in those portraits the settings belong to their own time, whereas here the backgrounds (especially those at Verona) are all of a previous age, and the effect of the contrast is even more striking.

But if he is right in his discovery of an Italian classical background in *Romeo and Juliet* and its visual transposition to the screen in an exquisite Renaissance pictorial key (with never an error of taste, lack of balance, or slackening of tone), does the story which Castellani has presented in the film, of the eternal love of Juliet and Romeo, taken almost word for word from Shakespeare's lines, succeed in giving life to a real cinematographic spectacle?

It is the question, the doubt which has already arisen in the minds of many regarding Olivier's films, his *Henry V*, his *Hamlet*, his *Richard III*. Are they theatre or cinema? For Castellani's *Romeo and Juliet* the answer is not one that can be given categorically. His fidelity to the text, his very discovery of an internal narrative scheme which, instead of giving him freedom of movement, has tied him rigidly to fixed rules, have obliged the director to follow a narrative tempo much closer to the theatre than to the cinema. Between the intervals of this tempo, however, his cinematographic invention has been able to give itself free rein with brilliant fertility and daring. It would be enough to mention, at the beginning, those close-ups of Verona, the Piazza delle Erbe market thronged with the many-colored crowd, a seething mass of brawling people; and then, soon after, the ball at the Capulets' house (all in red — only Juliet is in white and Romeo in black), which is an embroidery of precious harmonies, an exquisite page of cinema; and the friars on their knees singing plain song in the rose-tinted crypt of San Zeno, and Juliet's Byzantinesque funeral amid the resounding arches of the cathedral, the lights pouring down from the rose windows, the deep silence reigning all round; above all the silence, and the clear-cut, most felicitous sounds given out by the sound-track, the precise rhythm with which the notes of the music swell or fade away — all these are perfect elements in a perfect cinematographic poem, all calling forth true lyrical emotion.

And even when less open scenes do not allow the director's inventive power such scope (because they are

duets on the balcony or close dialogues between father and daughter or the meetings in Father Lorenzo's cell), we notice that the language of the cinema is always trying to assert itself, even within the theatrical speeches, either with a shot seen foreshortened from the bottom of a passage (so that the characters are all on different levels, as on a staircase), or with a continual changing of the positions of the actors and the angles from which they are seen (as in the duet, on the balcony, all played between the arches of a four-light mullioned window and the continually changing perspective of a marble staircase).

Later on, however, drawn by observation of reality, in *I sogni nel cassetto* (*Dreams in the Drawer*) Castellani was to give us a film of much more modest proportions, marked here and there, perhaps, by excessive romanticism, but in any case glowing with a kindly sympathy for the most ordinary characters of everyday life and for their trials and their problems. As if he regretted so much indulgence towards the tender side, however, Castellani now made a tough study of the problem of women in prison, composing in *Nella città l'inferno* (*Hell in Town*), with the leading role quite devastatingly played by the great Anna Magnani, a fresco of vast proportions, so tense in its dramatic moments as to be almost unbearable. In fact, someone felt bound to criticize him for the lack of balance and proportion proper to the atmosphere of harrowing tension.

The social present, to which Castellani had rarely condescended, sees him engaged in *Il brigante* (*The Brigand*), a film drawn from a novel by Giuseppe Berto set in a Calabria convulsed by class changes. The story finds in him a careful and accurate narrator, now polemical, now inspired, not always able, however, to impose a harmonious unity on the narration nor to keep the often epic atmosphere of the film clear of certain errors of taste and style, certain dramatic novelties which smack not so much of exasperation as of mere exaggeration.

These errors are particularly noticeable as regards the scenario which, with the weaknesses peculiar to overlong stories taken from novels too closely packed with incident, gives us characters who are often a little vague and only roughly sketched or who, although firmly and clearly drawn, do not always find their happiest place in the course of the story.

As regards the direction, however, the film claims a well-deserved attention, above all for certain choral sequences on which Castellani has lavished dramatic tension and realistic rigor in order to bring home to us the occupation of the estates, for example, or the cowed resignation of the peasants' lives in their homes or in the village square waiting for work; sequences, all of them, composed in a style in which the refinement of a rare and cleverly polished image blends with a dry, sincere respect for real facts, and with a rhythm which nearly always manages to remain nimble and free, with the tempo of a Western ballad and the verve of an epic poem.

But the same unevennesses of style and the same contradictions of inspiration were to appear again recently in *Mare matto* (*Mad Sea*), where Castellani, returning to the gay themes of *E' primavera* (*Springtime*) and choosing the lives of seafarers for his subjects, tried to achieve humorous and moving effects at the same time — with success only in some of the settings and in the highly colored, racy drawing of some minor characters.

Formalism seems to predominate over the humanity of the themes in Romeo and Juliet, notwithstanding the learned rigor with which Castellani has undertaken the " reading " of the Shakespearean text. But the film remains an example of a most noble pictorial splendor, especially as regards the transposition onto the cinematographic screen of the distinctive features and style of the finest Italian Renaissance painting.

Renato Castellani

GIULIETTA E ROMEO - ROMEO AND JULIET

Laurence Harvey, Susan Shantall, Flora Robson, Enzo Fieramonte (Universal-cine, 1954).

51

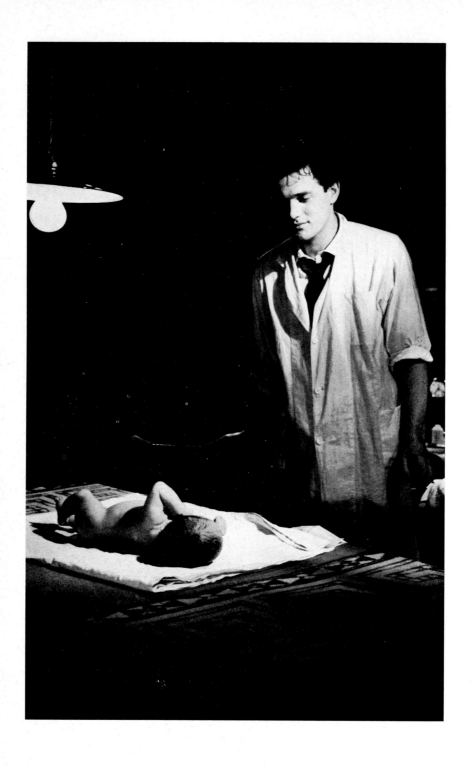

Renato Castellani

I SOGNI NEL CASSETTO
DREAMS IN THE DRAWER

Lea Massari, Enrico Pagani, Cosetta
Greco, Lilla Brignone, Sergio Tofano
(Rizzoli Film - Francinex, 1956).

Dreams in the Drawer, directs Castellani towards middle-class comedy,
redeemed only by a certain warmth in the images, which are particularly successful in the description of a city — Pavia — and the student
world. For the most part, however, these images are little more than
ends in themselves.

Renato Castellani

NELLA CITTÀ L'INFERNO - HELL IN TOWN

Anna Magnani, Giulietta Masina, Myriam Bru, Cristina Gajoni, Saro Urzi
(Riama Film, 1958).

After a realistic evocation of the world of women's prisons (in Hell in Town), in The Brigand Castellani returns to the open-air realism of Two Pennies Worth of Hope, permeated, this time, by sociopolemical as well as literary influences.

Renato Castellani

IL BRIGANTE - THE BRIGAND

Adelmo di Fraia, Francesco Seminario, Serena Vergano, Mario Jerard, Anna Filippini (Cineriz, 1961).

Renato Castellani

IL BRIGANTE - THE BRIGAND

Adelmo di Fraia, Francesco Seminario,
Serena Vergano, Mario Jerard, Anna
Filippini (Cineriz, 1961).

The images in The Brigand show us a Castellani once more careful
to express reality and to draw from all of it the most polished visual
suggestions. But here his story does not succeed either from the point
of view of harmony or balance; it is disappointing, too, because of the
excessive number of themes (for the most part left unresolved) and
the facile psychological similarity of its characters.

Renato Castellani

Mare matto - Mad sea

Gina Lollobrigida, Jean Paul Belmondo, Tomas Milian, Odoardo Spadaro (Lux - Vides - Films Ariane, 1963).

The same narrative disorder is found in Mad Sea, but, unlike The Brigand, since it is made up of different episodes, there is more excuse for its irregularities of style, climate, and rhythm. Its partiality for farce, however, is excessive and, in spite of one decidedly dramatic episode, it seems to take Castellani back to the somewhat easygoing days of Springtime.

Luigi Comencini

Born in Salò on June 8, 1916.

Principal films:

Tutti a casa; A cavallo della tigre; La ragazza di Bube; La mia signora; 3 notti d'Amore (an episode); Le Bambole (an episode); Il Compagno Don Camillo.

At a time when neorealism was merely gloomy, Luigi Comencini made the first in a series of films which were to be particularly successful: *Bread, Love, and Dreams.*

It was a sincere work, springing directly out of the rural setting in which it was placed, pervaded with hilarity and sentiment in accordance with the best Italian tradition. Later on, indulging in comic themes, he seemed to degenerate into farce in *I mariti in città (Husbands in Town),* but he retrieved himself by his interpretation, in ironical vein and with a certain polemical resentment, of the events of the 8th of September in *Tutti a casa (Back Home),* a film only in appearance aiming at caricature, in reality pervaded by human notes of a certain vigor, and told in a dry, dignified language, in no way favorable to the conventional image.

A more serious undertaking, too, was his most recent film, *La ragazza di Bube (Bebo's Girl),* very faithfully adapted from Carlo Cassola's novel and handled with particular warmth, above all from a stylistic point of view. The relation between the two protagonists, in fact, especially at the beginning, is arranged and then resolved with rigorous economy and with a concentration on essentials so harsh and severe as not to leave room for pauses, repetitions, or lingering, but, instead, with a rhythm which, always taut and sustained, runs on with limpid ease, keeping the two principal characters constantly in the foreground.

The emotional climate also is handled with care, because, although he does not slavishly follow the ways in which neorealism treated those first days of the immediate postwar period on which the action of the novel is based, he expresses the atmosphere of that time — the Americans, the partisans, the echoes in the provinces of the referendum of the 2nd of June, the hard years of reconstruction and the distress still prevailing — with sympathetic accuracy and an original way of setting things in relief all his own. He obtains attractive dramatic effects with chorus groupings so severely controlled that they never crowd out the protagonists, but, rather, act as a foil to enhance their coloring and precision. Later on, however, when the psychological contradictions in the text and its lack of balance between literature and realism (which was remarked at the time even by the critics most lenient towards Cassola) become more evident, Comencini has not succeeded in overcoming the negative weight of the story he set out from, and the film becomes more motiveless, more conventional, more static and monotonous in the narrative, even surrendering the field to some situations which are either too sentimental or too rhetorical. The result is that the story as a whole is rather disjointed and lacking in unity, not only on the aesthetic plane but also from the point of view of spectacle.

Comencini gives comedy a frequently polemical twist, with a balance and narrative gusto often particularly felicitous. He showed this in Back Home, in which the human aspect of the events of the 8th of September 1943, although in an intentionally caricaturist vein, was thrown into charming relief.

Luigi Comencini

TUTTI A CASA – BACK HOME

Alberto Sordi, Eduardo De Filippo, Serge Reggiani, Martin Balsam, Alex Nicol, Carla Gravina, Didi Perego (Dino De Laurentiis Cinemat., 1960).

Caricature, light comedy, but once again a warm, sincere humanity is found in Astride the Tigress, where Comencini's language becomes even more alive to the needs of a certainly elegant, if not exquisite, form in evoking definite places.

Luigi Comencini

A CAVALLO DELLA TIGRE - ASTRIDE THE TIGRESS

Nino Manfredi, Mario Adorf, Valeria Moriconi, Gian Maria Volontè, Raymond Bussières (Titanus, 1961).

Luigi Comencini

LA RAGAZZA DI BUBE - BEBO'S GIRL

Claudia Cardinale, George Chakiris, Marc Michel, Emilio Esposito (Lux - Ultra - Vides, 1964).

In evoking a period, and once again a particular setting, Bebo's Girl is successful because, often overcoming the unevennesses of a not always felicitous literary text, it not only puts on the screen two convincing, firmly drawn characters, but, from the photographic point of view, gives a very fresh and original picture of the immediate postwar period, the life of the partisans and of a certain country village world in the Tuscan Maremma — a picture derived from neorealism, but filtered through more personal and direct visual experiences.

GIUSEPPE DE SANTIS

Born in Fondi on February 11, 1917.

Principal films:

Caccia tragica; Riso amaro; Non c'è pace tra gli ulivi; Roma ore 11; Un marito per Anna Zaccheo; Giorni d'amore; Uomini e lupi; La strada lunga un anno; Italiani brava gente.

Giuseppe De Santis has always remained faithful to the earnest path of neorealism: in *Uomini e lupi* (*Men and Wolves*), in which, however, more than elsewhere he has indulged in a certain formalism which at times develops to the prejudice of the characters' humanity; and in *La strada lunga un anno* (*Year-Long Road*), a sort of ballad, now polemical, now ironical, in which the social themes often appear in the foreground altogether to the prejudice of the poetry, but which, as regards imagery, pictorial composition, harmony, and visual balance, must be considered a rare page of representational cinema.

It has a force, more than anything, a dramatic body and dryness, spoiled only by the longwindedness of the story, which only at certain moments is really well-knit and to the point.

Nor can his *Giorni d'amore* (*Days of Love*) (1954), a film almost on the level of comedy, be altogether forgotten: a rustic, but not dramatic, paraphrase of *Romeo and Juliet*, or rather of *Two Pennies' Worth of Hope*, worked out in the half-rural, half-sentimental climate of the rosy realism of *Pane amore e gelosia* (*Bread, Love and Jealousy*).

In his treatment of it, De Santis has not given us his pet social themes, but, considering the intentionally light tone of the story, he has kept himself pretty much on the surface: the characters are thus hardly sketched and do not go beyond a simple delineation, and the situations in which they figure are not always linked by a convincing narrative logic. There is, however, something in the film deserving of attention: it is the easy but fragrant breath of the countryside which spontaneously pervades the whole story, in a pleasing succession of colorful images often recalling, in their composition, the delicate charm of water-color and tempera landscapes.

Though a neorealist, De Santis has always been very careful of form too, at times in a negative sense, when the photography triumphs over the authenticity of the themes dealt with; but he often achieves a happy meeting point between a refined and polished photography and the tortured humanity of the characters — precisely as in Men and Wolves.

Giuseppe De Santis

UOMINI E LUPI - MEN AND WOLVES

Silvana Mangano, Yves Montand, Pedro Armendariz, Guido Celano (Titanus, 1956).

The pictorial composition here, in Year — Long Road, seems to take its inspiration directly from Breugel; it has the same harmony in the groups, the same precision in the single figures, the same impalpable airiness of pictorial textures. But from the narrative point of view, the film is patchy and tired, only occasionally enlivened by real, substantial sequences.

Giuseppe De Santis

LA STRADA LUNGA UN ANNO
YEAR LONG ROAD

Massimo Girotti, Silvana Pampanini, Eleonora Rossi Drago (Zagreb, Film, 1958).

Giuseppe De Santis

ITALIANI BRAVA GENTE
ITALIANS, GOOD PEOPLE

Arthur Kennedy, Gianna Prokhorenkho,
Raffaele Pisu, Tatiana Samoilova, Andrea Checchi, Riccardo Cucciolla, Gri-
gori Michailov, Nino Vingelli, Gino Pernice, Lev Prigunev, Peter Falk (Galatea - Coronet - Mos Film, 1964).

With Italians, Good People De Santis offers a new choral film with ambitious intentions which are not always realized in the attempt to reconstruct a historical period and atmosphere.

VITTORIO DE SICA

Born in Sora (Frosinone) on July 7, 1902.

Principal films:

Rose scarlatte; Maddalena zero in condotta; Teresa Venerdì; Un garibaldino al convento; I bambini ci guardano; La porta del cielo; Sciuscià; Ladri di biciclette; Miracolo a Milano; Umberto D.; Stazione Termini; L'oro di Napoli; La ciociara; Il giudizio universale; Boccaccio 70 (an episode); I sequestrati di Altona; Il boom; Ieri oggi e domani; Matrimonio all'italiana.

After the success of *Miracle in Milan*, Vittorio De Sica has followed paths which are often contradictory; for, while holding firmly to that lyrical inspiration from which his best films took their origin, he has welcomed suggestions which are not always consistent, wandering off along roads which hardly lead back to a unified conception of the cinema. The results are sometimes just as felicitous, but at times rather debatable.

His collaboration with Cesare Zavattini continues without interruption, empowering him to go on deepening the world of contemporary ideas and argument, solidly embedding it in the richest lode of the greatest literature and of the most modern and socially engaged culture.

An instance, however, of the enduring strength of this collaboration was given us in *Umberto D.*, a film which, although disjointed in places, allowed De Sica to work out, in terms of the cinema, the subject suggested to him by Zavattini with altogether exemplary sequences. To tell the truth, the subject is not always very plausible, based as it is on the drama of a poor pensioner to whom human beings regularly behave like wild animals — unlike the animals which, on the contrary, show almost human feelings towards him. But why are Umberto D.'s antagonists such beastly creatures, and whatever was the idea in telling us about it? The film does not give a convincing answer, although Zavattini's story, while describing a modest slice of life episode, hoped to achieve a literary prospect where reality and imagination could comfortably merge in a world of hallucination and make-believe. In that case the unkindness would have had an explanation of its own, and perhaps the description of it might have bordered on poetry.

De Sica, however, has faithfully reproduced the episode, and his direction, true to life in all details, has often achieved a limpid and sensitive air. But at times

he has misunderstood the inner reasons for its absurdity, falling into contrived and uncalled-for situations, helped in this by a text overburdened with narrative matter which is not always very clear.

Nevertheless, to his honor there are some fine sequences which deserve the warmest praise, beginning with the maid waking up in the morning, where minute observation of detail achieves real human effects of the most sensitive kind.

The following year, 1953, *Stazione Termini* (*Indiscretion of an American Wife*) appeared, a film which, although based on the same realistic presuppositions as De Sica's other films, is weakened from the outset by an encounter, at the time still premature, with the cinema of Hollywood, which provided not only financial backing, but also two of its celebrated stars of the moment, Jennifer Jones and Montgomery Clift.

Mary, a young American from Philadelphia, comes to Rome to stay with a sister for a while. Here, although she has a husband and daughter in America, she falls in love with an Italian, Giovanni, and for a month forgets everything in his company. One day, suddenly seized with remorse as she remembers her distant family, she decides to leave. Giovanni overtakes her at the station and tries in vain to persuade her to stay. The coming and going of the passengers, the trains, the little daily incidents in a big railway station, form the background to this tense dialogue between the two who, although both want the same thing (to remain together), will part in the end.

This dialogue, at times dramatic, tender, violent, and romantic, represents the whole film, which is made to last exactly as long as the action. When he has to put the man and woman opposite each other in the pain and passion of their love, De Sica shows himself a sensitive psychologist and an exact and careful observer;

but when he puts the noisy setting of the station around the central drama (with an atmosphere, either indifferent or inattentive, which, following the celebrated example of *Devil in the Flesh*, naturally had to be in complete contrast with the state of mind of the two protagonists), he simply creates a modest gallery of human types, often drawn with a certain lack of precision.

Moreover, the intentional and too realistic respect for the unities of time and place in one way seems to concentrate the dramatic tension, but in another, since it requires a great deal of explanatory dialogue about what has happened before, causes too many halts in many minor episodes which, more often than not, appear rather artificial.

However, even though here and there one may be disconcerted by the strangeness of the film and its excessive pauses, one cannot help being emotionally convinced by the painful atmosphere hanging over the lovers' agonizing good-bye, and by the bitter intensity with which the two American stars, ably directed toward a realistic interpretation, succeed in giving expression and dramatic consistency to their despair.

More in De Sica's line — the De Sica who has always found the sincerest and warmest occasions for his inspiration in his own southern origins — is *The Gold of Naples*, based on some short stories by Giuseppe Marotta. These are built round a whole gallery of characters, sometimes eccentric, sometimes odd, but always, in their melancholy and their dramatic character, extremely human and well-drawn. Equally human and well-drawn is the Neapolitan setting around them, full of strength and vitality, even though devoid of gaiety.

The film (here, too, the screenplay is by Cesare Zavattini) retraces five of these stories with an almost twilight tone and rhythm which, at least in part, dampens the ardor the author of the stories had given them.

The first episode relates how Don Saverio, a silly fellow, at last succeeds in forcibly freeing himself from a bully who for years had planted himself in his house, terrorizing his wife, his children, and himself. Don Saverio musters up courage only when the bully is ill, but even afterwards, when the latter comes back and says he is in excellent health, the family, who have now overcome the terror he had struck into them, bravely stand together against him.

This story is perhaps the most complete of them all; it is told with perfect timing, and its setting of poor alleys, poor houses, poor squares, is more concrete, alive, and effective than any other. Totò in the part of the silly fellow gives it added color: in his interpretation of the part he is careful to give first a balanced expression of the weak man's mental torture and then his still timid, fear-ridden revolt.

The second episode is just as lively, but perhaps indulges too much in caricature. It is the tragi-comedy of a valuable ring a beautiful woman has left in her lover's house, but which her husband, a pizza cook, thinks he has cooked in the pizzas: there follows a frantic search for all the people who bought pizzas that day.

There is plenty of color, plenty of rhythm, and plenty of poise, but it is all pitched on a high note and is often perilously near falling from comedy into farce, even though most amusing farce.

The third episode is a simple but exquisite intermezzo. A crazy old aristocrat plays *scopone* with the porter's son and gets furious when he loses. It has the shining merit of a card game which relies for its effect, amid silences, pauses, and grimaces, simply on De Sica's mischievous interpretation and the delightful acting of a sulky child.

Nocturnal, decadent, almost Gozzinian, is the episode of Teresa, the prostitute a rich man marries simply in order to punish himself for having been the unwitting cause of a girl's suicide. It is interwoven with keen psychological insights and even irony, but it is hardly able to achieve a real dramatic consistency. The last episode is only an epilogue: it gives us the figure of a "wisdom vendor," a guitar player who is visited at his house by people anxious for his advice.

But have all these episodes strung together anything in common, a definite note, a value poetically transcending them? Perhaps it is Naples, the people, the pain, the scant though so much celebrated gaiety. But in spite of De Sica's stylistic skill, in spite of the brilliance of a language which is able to give life and warmth even to the stones of a road, it is difficult to believe in it altogether, as if everything remained at the level, perfect but external, of an exercise.

Two years later (1956), we find De Sica returning, perhaps for the last time (in *The Roof*), to a minute, urbane realism, pervaded by a sentimentality which is, in spite of the harshness of its polemics, close to that of De Amicis, telling us the story of the adventures of Luisa and Natale in their desperate hunt for a roof over their heads after their wedding.

In describing these adventures, he has taken particular care with the central figures, drawing with affectionate insight Luisa's fiery, somewhat domineering and headstrong nature, and, in contrast, Natale, hesitating, often intimidated, but at any rate sincere and good-hearted. Carefully measuring their reactions, he studies all their psychological developments, attunes their characters to the situations in which they find themselves with a serene sense of proportion, and tries to win understanding and sympathy for them. For instance, there are the scenes at the beginning where they get married in circumstances of the most abject poverty, and then rush off to tell her father who was opposed to the marriage, and then, later, when the first troubles begin in her father's house, or when, in the dead of night, they hastily build the unauthorized house in which they will go and live.

Certainly, the poverty of the story shows through when it is not covered up by dramatic intensity, but this does not happen very often. The secondary figures are, in general, barely outlined, and some are quite pointless or appear simply as "presences" — the group represented by the bricklayers, for example, who work together to help the couple build the house, or the group representing the relatives. If their psychological values had been redeemed by an atmosphere maintained on a constantly moving and poetical level, we should have accepted them more readily and they would have persuaded us to follow Natale and Luisa's adventures with more sympathy.

Even so, however, in spite of the flimsiness of the story and a lack of lively ideas and episodes, the film has some good points as regards form, and deserves to be remembered for its polished style and sound technique.

After four years of silence as a director, in 1960 De Sica found the happiest means of applying his realistic creed to literature when he adapted *Two Women*, one of Moravia's most celebrated novels, for the screen.

The novel gave us the terrible picture of the last months of the war in Lazio, seen through the eyes of an ex-peasant woman. Evacuated from Rome into the mountains of Fondi with her twelve-year-old daughter, after a hard struggle against famine and hunger, when liberation came she had the tragedy of seeing her daughter become indifferent to goodness after they both were raped by a band of marauding Moroccan troops. The woman, driven by want, went as far as to steal, but then sorrow over the death of somebody dear to her and, above all, the thought of all the sorrow left by the war, cleansed her and helped her to return to the path of honesty.

The strength of the novel was in the pitiless description of the privations the war inflicted on civilians, as shown in the character of the peasant woman who tried to cope with these privations, sometimes greedily and sometimes with a rough, sincere generosity which enabled her, in the end, to surmount the hardest trials.

The film avoids putting the accent directly on the protagonist's character or on the change in the girl's character after she is raped by the Moroccans; hence it refuses to accept the idea that suffering purifies, which had been the keynote of Moravia's story. The theme of the film, briefly summarized from the main narrative lines of the novel, is the war, with the anxiety attending the evacuation, the fear of the Germans, the precarious safety of the early days after the liberation. The woman is at the center of the action, not so much in order to pass judgment on this war, but to suffer it all in her own flesh and blood and her daughter's and to be sustained only by a desperate instinct of self-preservation.

In these sufferings the film writes its barest, leanest, most desolate pages, beginning with the terrible one, although streaked with dry reserve, of the Moroccans raping the girl and her mother. Perhaps, the subject matter being what it is, we should have expected a deeper sense of tragedy, an expressive violence to commemorate in every image the anguish, the horror, and the terror of those days, especially as felt by two frail women.

But De Sica has preferred a calmer, more collected descriptive tone, sustained almost on a single note, and, except for the opening scene of the bombardment of Rome and the raping scene, he has maintained a tranquil, limpid style, aiming only at a realistic presentation of those desolate mountain and country settings and that excited chorus of peasants and evacuees against whom the impetuous simplicity of the heroine stands out in high relief.

Less convincing as a film, but equally worthy of note as regards the direction is *The Last Judgment*, on a subject by Cesare Zavattini.

What last judgment? The real, mysterious, terrible one described by St. John? No, simply a laughing matter, something between satire, ballet, and the grotesque.

It is set in Naples, the city where anything is possible, where one may laugh about death and weep over life. People are getting ready for day when the angel announces a grand ball, and everybody (or nearly everybody) seems delighted with it: the young because it will give them the chance for lovers' meetings, the old because they will be able to carry on some profitable business

there. But suddenly a mighty voice from on high intones the warning: "At 6 p.m. the Last Judgment will begin!" At first, no one pays any attention, but then, since the voice continues, even those who had thought it was some publicity stunt realize their mistake and are seized with terror, displaying a variety of different reactions on which a highly colored series of episodes is gradually built up. De Sica presents them in such a way that the whole story, set against the realistic backround of a Naples grim with fear and winter, almost creates the atmosphere of a metaphysical fable, at times close to nightmare and dreams, at other times open to comedy, farce, and ballet. It is a ballet which gives us its lightest moments (almost à la Clair) in the episode of a diplomat at grips with a servant he mistreats; a ballet which, changing into dance and "cantata," breaks up into broad choral rhythms in the episode of an American racist who, after a repentant lullaby for a little Negro, adorns the episodes which follow with song and music. Alongside the ballet there is caricature, and there is sentimental, melancholy, and moralizing comedy; resolved now and again with an attempt at narrative which, especially in the second part (too feeble after the vigorous opening preparation), slows up a little the onward sweep of the story. This defect, however, is often amply redeemed by the care with which De Sica — with one of his most sustained and fertile pieces of directing — has built round the story a rich Neapolitan setting made up of alleys, cul-de-sacs, and crossroads dark with rain, and the liveliness with which he has been able to give even the characters a human aspect charged with meaning.

Thus, in spite of its narrative hesitations, the film is a success because (if for no other reason) it represents the first attempt, with excellent results, to introduce the grotesque of the theatre into the cinema.

After the gay, somewhat coarse farce of the episode, "The Raffle" (1961), inserted into the film of episodes, *Boccaccio '70*, De Sica in 1962 tackles an author rather foreign to his habits and mentality, Jean-Paul Sartre. Although his adaptation of *The Prisoners of Altona* is open to criticism, it nevertheless remains a testimony to his worth as a director.

The Prisoners of Altona was certainly not Sartre's soundest play, but it was among those which tackled the subjects, so much debated, of collective responsibility and the justification of one's own acts to oneself and to posterity with the most unflinching rigor and the most merciless logic. Its central figure was the son of a powerful German industrialist who, during the war, had not hesistated to become a torturer. When he returned home, the nightmare of punishment and the contrast between his destructive fanaticism and the rapid rebirth of his country had led him to shut himself up in voluntary imprisonment in the family villa, where only a sister, tied to him by a confused relationship, visits him. The father, about to die from an incurable disease, wants to pull him out of this isolation, now bordering on madness, so he asks his younger son's wife to bring him face to face with his responsibilities. She explains to him, among other things, the truth about German reconstruction which, in order to justify his renunciation of life, he wished neither to become aware of nor to acknowledge. But when the young man realizes the truth and sees it in such violent contradiction to his past crimes, he choses to commit suicide with his father.

Sartre made use of these characters to feed his polemics against dictatorship, tyranny, and selfishness and, through a wealth of symbols, to bolster up his usual existentialist theories with a style which, in spite of its sententious wordiness and its predilection for long monologues and prolix perorations, often succeeded in holding the audience — and this, too, because of the singularly cinematographic rhythms with which the many flashbacks to the protagonist's past were dealt with.

Could these rhythms have been some help to a person who, without worrying about certain obscurities in the text, was preparing to translate it onto the screen? At first sight one would have said yes, but to judge from the adaptation proposed to De Sica by scriptwriters Abby Mann and Cesare Zavattini, they have been led to say no. Why? Why have the two scriptwriters solved by means of dialogue alone, and that in the manner of the theatre, those very flashbacks which Sartre had dealt with visually, and again why, wishing to shorten and, essentially, explain it, have they cut the drama so much to the bone that the characters have, on the one hand, lost their real tragic dimensions and, on the other, have been transformed into facile symbols, used only to express outward and immediate contrasts?

The result is a story which is almost more suited to the stage than the text of the drama itself, in some places more static and in others, in spite of the explanations and the often exaggerated and uncalled-for narrative variants (as in the finale and the intellectualist digressions on the stage of the *Berliner Ensemble*), more obscure than the original work. Of great merit, however, is the directing, or rather, the *mise en scène*, of Vittorio De Sica: alive, modern, constantly sustained by an inner need for linguistic renewal; as witness the initial shot which, in an atmosphere of Nibelungian twilight, takes us into the secret anguish of the old despot who is impotent before the sentence of death he has received, or some of the sequences where the fixed scheme of the theatre, hardly brought to life by the scenario, seems conquered and redeemed by the sheer rhythmic play of the photography.

After *Il boom* (once again from a script by Zavattini) with Alberto Sordi in the leading part — a return to the concrete themes of current affairs from which he has always drawn his best poetical inspirations — De Sica has recently (1964) given us a comedy, a gay episode film, *Yesterday, Today, and Tomorrow*. In this, although he only displays an easy zest for farce, he has pulled off a delightful success in the field of light entertainment, a field which only in appearance is open to all.

In the same vein as those other Neapolitan period pieces which he did so successfully, De Sica gives us *Marriage Italian Style*, based on Eduardo De Filippo's much renowned *Filumena Marturano*. The film is, by and large, popular in style, rich in all the devices of the spectacle, fulfilling enough in the passion and excitement of its tale to captivate the balcony if not the unreserved esteem of the critics.

Notwithstanding the contradictions of a path often hindered by retrograde steps, the drag of literary texts, and contaminations between his own warm inspiration and the arid polemics of others, De Sica remains one of the most significant directors in the cinema: above all for his technical skill which, when not hindered by suggestions foreign to him, becomes style — a firm, vigorous, exemplary style.

Vittorio De Sica

UMBERTO D.

C. Battisti, Maria Pia Casilio (G. Amato 1952).

Umberto D. is a new "Roman symphony" by De Sica. His visual language, finished and perfect in itself, never overwhelms the character; rather, it surrounds him with such dramatic circumstances that the setting in its turn becomes a character, emphasizes, determines, and explains states of mind, at times with very apt psychological consequences.

If Terminal Station is an experiment rather far from De Sica's inspiration, notwithstanding the linguistic zeal he has displayed in it, The Gold of Naples reopens the series of realistic stories, rendered warmer, more colorful, more human by a literary atmosphere which, directly based on reality, was bound to be a better source of inspiration for De Sica.

Vittorio De Sica

L'ORO DI NAPOLI - THE GOLD OF NAPLES

Sophia Loren, Giacomo Furia, Paolo Stoppa, Eduardo De Filippo, Totò, Silvana Mangano, Ubaldo Maestri, Vittorio De Sica, Luciano Rondinella, Tina Pica (Ponti-De Laurentiis, 1954).

Two Women is De Sica's last neorealist page which, although based on a literary text, the novel by Alberto Moravia, succeeds solely by virtue of its poetical fidelity to the most concrete reality, in a visual climate which filters the lessons of Shoeshine through a photography which is never an end in itself.

Vittorio De Sica

LA CIOCIARA - TWO WOMEN

Sophia Loren, Jean Paul Belmondo, Eleonora Brown, Raf Vallone, Carlo Ninchi, Renato Salvatori (Champion Film, 1960).

Vittorio De Sica

Il giudizio universale
The last judgment

Alberto Sordi, Melina Mercouri, Fernandel, Nino Manfredi, Silvana Mangano, Ernest Borgnine, Jack Palance, Renato Rascel, Paolo Stoppa, Don Jaime De Mora y Aragon, Mike Bongiorno, Vittorio Gassman (Dino De Laurentiis Cinemat, S.p.A., 1961).

Fable, grotesquery, fantasy, and folklore are the typical ingredients of The Last Judgment, definitely a work of refinement as regards the direction, but, from a narrative point of view, contradictory and debatable.

Vittorio De Sica

BOCCACCIO '70 (La riffa) - (THE RAFFLE)

Sophia Loren (Concordia Cinemat - Cineriz - Francinex Gray Film, 1961).

"The Raffle": De Sica amusing himself with short stories, in genuine caricaturist vein. The color helps to quench the realist inspiration in favor of an easy, almost extemporaneous spectacle.

Vittorio De Sica
I SEQUESTRATI DI ALTONA
THE PRISONERS OF ALTONA

Sophia Loren, Maximilian Schell, Fredric March, Robert Wagner, François Prevost (Titanus - Société Générale de Cinématographie, 1962).

The Prisoners of Altona is not really a De Sica film. He is responsible for little more than the mise en scène, master as always of a secure technique.

Vittorio De Sica

Il boom - Boom

Alberto Sordi, Gianna Maria Canale, Silvio Battistini, Ettore Geri, Elena Nicolai (Dino De Laurentiis Cinemat. 1963).

Boom is satirical comedy on the most topical themes of our daily life. But tackled with the levity of a ballet which seems to delight by its superficiality.

Vittorio De Sica

IERI, OGGI, DOMANI
YESTERDAY, TODAY, AND TOMORROW

Sophia Loren, Marcello Mastroianni,
Tina Pica, Gianni Ridolfi, Aldo Giuffrè,
Tecla Scarano, Agostino Salvietti
(Champion Film, 1964).

Farce again: Yesterday, Today, and Tomorrow. It is written by no less
a partnership than Eduardo De Filippo and Cesare Zavattini, but,
notwithstanding De Sica's always skillful direction, the film does not
rise above the level of facile spectacle, out simply to make money.

Marriage Italian Style, based on the comedy Filumena Marturano by Eduardo De Filippo, is a skillfully directed movie which, however, caters too much to the taste of the popular public. It is undoubtedly an impressive film of its kind, capitalizing on the dramatic qualities of the tale and on the popularity of the main actors.

Vittorio De Sica

MATRIMONIO ALL'ITALIANA
MARRIAGE ITALIAN STYLE

Sophia Loren, Marcello Mastroianni, Aldo Puglisi, Marilu Tolo, Tecla Scarano.

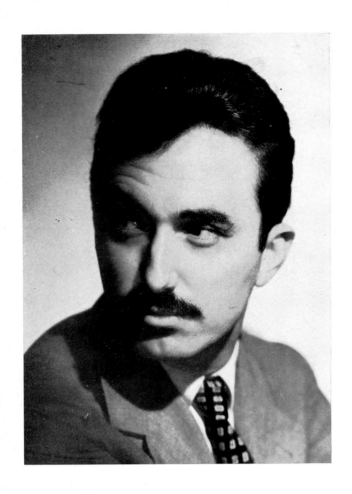

LUCIANO EMMER

Born in Milan on June 19, 1918.

Principal films:

Domenica d'agosto; Parigi è sempre Parigi; Le ragazze di Piazza di Spagna; Terza liceo; Amore in città (an episode); Camilla; Il bigamo; La ragazza in vetrina.

Luciano Emmer is a maker of documentaries who has undeniably held a place of some importance in the cinema not with one but with several films. After winning the approval of all the critics with his documentaries on painting, made in collaboration with Enrico Gras, he soon made his mark with stories, generally in episode form, with a predominant vein of affable cordiality, half sentimental, half humorous.

Among these, after the pleasant first film *Domenica di agosto* (*August Sunday*), came *Parigi è sempre Parigi,* (*Paris Is Always Paris*), an easy, ironic little comedy, perhaps just a little too sketchy. Then *Le ragazze di Piazza di Spagna* (*The Girls of Piazza di Spagna*), and *Terzo Liceo* (*Third Lyceum*), gracefully constructed on the world of youth and adolescence, its dreams, disappointments, and amorous adventures; *Camilla* in which, perhaps for the first time, Emmer focused on a leading character with some depth and body, in the person of a worthy maid who rules the destinies of a rather crazy family; and *The Bigamist* in which, notwithstanding some unnecessarily farcical excess, he tried his hand at caricature.

But his most serious and sustained film is unquestionably *La ragazza in vetrina* (*The Girl in the Shop Window*) on the life of the Italian miners in Holland — built around a stimulating clash of personalities, worked out with inspired sympathy, and, as regards the setting, with a brilliant visual language.

88

Luciano Emmer

Terza liceo - Junior year high school

Isabella Redi, Anna Maria Sandri, Roberta Primavera, Giulia Rubino, Giovanna Tuzi, Cristina Carere, Ferdinando Cappabianca, Ugo Arnoldi (Incim, 1953).

89

Emmer's best film remains The Girl in the Shop Window: for its well-rounded characters, the telling drama of its story, and its careful style — the fruit, this time, of Emmer's best experience in documentary films.

Luciano Emmer

LA RAGAZZA IN VETRINA
THE GIRL IN THE SHOP WINDOW

Lino Ventura, Marina Vlady, Magali Noël, Bernard Fresson, Antonio Badas, Salvatore Lombardo, Giulio Mancini, Roger Bernard (Nepi Film - Sofidetip, Zodiaque Film, 1960).

FEDERICO FELLINI

Born in Rimini on January 20, 1920.

Principal films:

Lo sceicco bianco; I vitelloni; La strada; Il bidone; Le notti di Cabiria; La dolce vita; Boccaccio '70 (an episode); 8½; Giulietta degli spiriti.

Ever since the end of the war, the Italian middle classes had been waiting for their interpreter. In 1953, with *I vitelloni*, Federico Fellini showed he wanted to be this: and with such precision and such a clearly avowed intention, that he at once gripped the attention of the public as well as of the critics. A melancholy and nostalgic interpreter, of course, just as our middle classes are melancholy and nostalgic, but an interpreter, too, who is not adverse to irony and ridicule, but who, instead, makes use of them at once whenever melancholy and nostalgia seem to be carrying him too far towards the slippery slopes of sentimentalism and rhetoric.

The characters of *I vitelloni* reflect this very state of mind, Fellini's identical, reasoned oscillation between the two opposing sentiments of joy and sadness. They are called *vitelloni* because this is the term for those young men of good family who, in the provinces, spend their days in utter idleness, dividing their time beween the café, billiards, a walk, and the little society party. The monotony of provincial life has covered them with a dull blanket of boredom, has wrapped them in a veil of unconscious sadness from which they only emerge for some vaguer game. As a rule they are not yet married (marriage necessarily changes a good-for-nothing fellow into a man burdened with more definite responsibilities), and their love affairs alway smack of the adventure which

leaves no traces behind it, except when something serious happens. Fellini draws them all for us in clear, precise lines, and — although from the same visual angle as the *vitelloni* themselves — sharply distinguishes them from each other. Thus their histories glow with a deep human warmth; a gentle, very subtle poetry hovers over their lives, seen always with a sympathetic understanding which, through irony, if not actual satire, knows how to criticize morals in a friendly way, not rebuking but only putting forward suggestions.

There is no unevenness in the story or in the rhythm which serenely regulates its onward flow; nor does the directing show unevennesses because there is not a single part in the narrative — even the most difficult, the most scabrous, the most ordinary — which he is not able to express with extreme delicacy, and with such keen restraint (restraint in rhetoric, tears, discords, and laughter) that whenever a scene or character seems to be going too far, there is always an abrupt swerve in the opposite direction to restore the balance about to be lost.

And all this in an atmosphere — that of the Italian provincial citizen and bourgeoisie — which almost assumes the rank of a character for the trenchant terms and the precision with which every part of it is drawn, whether it be houses and squares at night, a Carnival masked ball, a Lenten dawn, a démodé café, a train departing, a beach, or a third-rate theatre.

The following year we see Fellini achieving more decidedly poetic aims in *La strada*, a film which, overcoming the fortuitousness of realistic observation, heads with firm decision towards the realms of fantasy and symbol. Gelsomina, the protagonist, is a shy, dreamy, starry-eyed girl who lives shut up in world of her own. The "things not seen" are more real for her than those that are. One day she becomes the workmate of Zampanò, a strolling mountebank, who is her exact opposite: he only believes in what he sees, and in an animal and brutish way. Although these two spend their days at close quarters in a gipsy wagon, there is no point of contact between them; a wall divides them the wall of brute matter in which the spirit can make no breach. Gelsomina, however, does not easily resign herself to the silence of Zampanò's soul. Behind the outward appearance of everything, she hears the sweet voice of a much more mysterious reality and tries to communicate her truer world to him, but her efforts are in vain and one day she would have been on the verge of giving up everything, if another strolling player, a mad tightrope walker nicknamed Crazy, had not revealed to her the only secret she did not yet know, that of herself. Like every creature on this earth, she too has some purpose — Crazy tells her — and for her "to have some purpose' means staying near Zampanò, even though she cannot understand why. Gelsomina listens to him and stays, with hope kindled anew, but shortly afterwards Zampanò kills Crazy in a brawl. The girl suddenly feels the bottom has dropped out of her secret world and goes mad. And Zampanò, on whom Gelsomina's wisdom never made the slightest impression, is now shaken out of his folly; indeed, he is so terror-stricken that he suddenly runs away, all by himself, with his wagon.

Years pass and one day Zampanò chances to hear that Gelsomina is dead. Her death opens the eyes of his mind to everything: to Gelsomina's life. the things in which Gelsomina believed and which he had never "seen." Now, through Gelsomina's eyes, Zampanò "sees" all those things, and the wall which imprisoned his soul suddenly collapses. Reality, after all, is not only what we see, but also, and above all, that other reality which, in the mystery of the invisible, gives it value, purpose, and meaning.

This is the conclusion Fellini arrives at by patiently constructing, entirely from within, the long, secret travail of his two characters: a conclusion which succeeds because of its high moral value and the ambitious aims with which the director works it out on the level of poetry, without any concessions to popular entertainment, in an atmosphere dominated solely by the unusual, always interpreted in a half-romantic, half-realistic vein, where the enchanted world of fable mingles with the rough, bleak world of fact.

After two experiments of a certain polemical value, but which disappoint here and there as regards the maturity of the style — *The Nights of Cabiria* and *Il bidone* — Fellini confronts the most topical themes of our times in *La dolce vita*. It is one of the strangest, most profound, and, in its way, most tragic films the Italian cinema has produced: a festival of all the falsities, mystifications, and corruptions of an age, a funereal portrait of a society, apparently still young and healthy, which, as

in mediaeval paintings, dances with Death without seeing it, a human comedy of a crisis which, as in Goya's pictures or Kafka's tales, is changing men into monsters without men having time to realize it.

Monsters, real monsters, that is what all these characters are, conjured up by the director on the basis of certain happenings reported in the press. The leading figure, or rather the one the author uses to introduce us into the infernal regions of our present-day *dolce vita*, is a journalist, a man come to Rome from the provinces, who soon forgets the home left behind him in order to plunge headlong into a semi-society profession which soon brings him into contact with all the city circles most in the public eye: the rich, the aristocrats, the film world, the intellectuals, the good-timers, but also, of course, the poor, the obscure, those who only know notoriety if they get mixed up in some sensational crime. He still has a little good left in him — a regret, perhaps, for lost virtue, for purity never recovered. But the life he leads, the circles he frequents, have now made him hard and cynical, incapable of avowing sincere love for a woman, ready instead to accept violent, passing adventures wherever he is offered them, and ready to adapt himself to the world he lives in, the vices he rubs shoulders with, the society of "monsters" he is now a member of.

Among the "monsters," those nearest to him, because of his profession, are the press photographers, always dancing a merciless, macabre ballet around evil, sorrow, and crime reports, indifferent to everything outside their trade. But equally macabre is the dance of the rich and of the aristocrats who are more broken down than their dilapidated castles. Yet both are incapable of finding in pleasure, orgies, and sex what they do not realize they need to fill the emptiness of which they are beginning to be afraid.

The one who does realize this emptiness — an intellectual who hitherto has toyed with the empty words of others like him — actually goes mad, kills his children and then himself: the one who stops halfway at the discovery plunges headlong into the flesh, but *hélas*, he has already read *tous les livres*, and he finds it as sad as his own sadness.

At the end of this pilgrimage among the "monsters," one ghastly dawn after an orgy the protagonist sees a real monster loom up on a beach, a horrible catch from the sea, very much like those which, when they appeared in the Middle Ages, were said to herald wars, plagues, and disasters. At the same time, it is true, he also meets a clean young girl who seems like the product of a different generation and perhaps — like Beatrice or Matilda — could sweeten the waters of his life. But our hero is not of those who will survive the flood, and notwithstanding the "sign" given him, we see him tagging after his "monsters" again, resuming with them the daily *danse macabre* in company with Death and the Devil.

Is it polemics, symbolism, allegory, or indictment? Nothing of the kind. Fellini has deliberately steered clear of the "thesis" film, has scrupulously avoided programmatic, rhetorical, or moralistic accents, and instead has chosen to describe for their contemporaries the "monsters" of today with the same participation and, we would say, the same connivance with which Baudelaire described to his reader (whom, as a matter of fact, he called *mon semblable, mon frère*) *les monstres glapissants, hurlants, grognants, rampants* who belonged to the *ménagerie infâme* of the vices of his day. And he has done it with a dramatic power, a vehemence, and a freshness of language which, notwithstanding the reservations necessary for the weakness of some episodes (when they are too emphasized, too frank or unpleasant), certainly place his film among the most "modern" works of art in the cinema. Fellini, in fact, has placed himself in the center of our contemporary disorder and has drawn from it, with disconcerting fullness, a huge choral assembly. His narration rejects logical steps, graduations, crescendos, and spectacular effects in the transitions; there are never heights and depths, concatenations, or links. A vision of this world of ours in perennial turmoil is reached with a sustained feverish rhythm, and all its many social and individual aspects are analysed in the giddy, anxious, desperate whirl of a dance we are all called to take part in — with a horrifying doom hanging over us.

"Dr. Antonio's Temptations" from the episode film, made in collaboration, *Boccaccio '70*, is a satirical, or rather, downright farcical parenthesis. In it Fellini tackles in an ironical vein the same themes he has confronted in his other films in a serious and polemical spirit. He amused himself too much, however, perhaps to amuse others too much, and the short film thus commends itself above all for the wonderful levity of a style which is now able to transform into cinema whatever it touches.

There followed a pause, perhaps caused by the preparation of one of the most discussed and most significant films of the last few years: *8½*. After fearing that with *La dolce vita* he could not get away from the death monsters hanging over our contemporary society, and with *The Nights of Cabiria* and *Il bidone*, that he could not succeed in overcoming the negative weight of the selfishness, hatred, and tyranny which crush and often destroy the men of today, Fellini here reaches the view that life is a holiday worth living in the company of others.

To reach this view he has laid himself bare, confessing publicly not only his private anguish, but also (simultaneously and symbolically) the travail he suffers as a creator, and, with a continual parallelism between the two terms, has told us the story of a man (who is also a cinema director) who is oppressed and obsessed to such a pitch by others — wife, friends, colleagues — that he only wishes to be alone, far away from everybody, incapable at the same time of organizing his own ideas, his own inspiration, and, therefore, of creating.

This man, Guido, has taken refuge in a spa in order to recover physically and put himself right morally, and also to make a film of which no one (himself included) really knows the subject, although the great producing machine, headed by the producer, has already been placed at his entire disposal. So, taking the cure, meditating, keeping at bay the cinema people who pester him for news, orders, and ideas, and in the meantime keeping at bay all the many women in his life he cannot bear any longer and whom, obviously, he has never succeeded in keeping at peace with each other (not to mention with himself), Guido tries to put a little order into his inner confusion. In reveries, memories, and dreams he tries to find the guiding thread of his existence (and also of his next film); applies himself anxiously to the pursuit of excitement and inspiration, fearful he has lost them forever; and finally, crushed by a sterility

which seems to smother every idea, broken by the collapse of his marriage (his wife, tired of his disorderly life and sickened by the lies he masks it with, wants to leave him), for a moment he thinks of suicide, and then, his mind made up, gives up creative activity, film, work, everything.

But at that moment (in a flash, like dull Zampanò on the beach, under the stars), he understands everything and, adopting a new attitude to the people in his life and the characters, as yet unexpressed, of his film, he accepts them as they are, without changing them or himself, and so at last no longer feels oppressed or rejected. "How right it is to accept you and love you, and how simple it is," he says now. And he who, in his reveries, had reached the point of seeing himself with a revolver aimed at his temple, he who, in his nightmares, always felt himself oppressed by others, almost buried in a coffin made by an indifferent or hostile neighbor, comes to call life a holiday and gladly asks those he had shunned before to live it with him, with no more selfishness and lies. ("Telling the truth that's he only way I feel alive.")

This confession is possibly autobiographical, but it is also the clear X-ray of a creative process (the film we see is "also" the filmed story of the preparation of a film which is then abandoned, followed by the decision to make another on different human lines). Fellini has told it with unforgettable photography, creating something which, all things considered, is perhaps not a film — in the ordinary, traditional sense of the term — but is certainly cinema, pure cinema.

The story is told throughout on two levels: the literal level, which tells us of the doubts and perplexities of Guido the cinema director, and the symbolical level, which portrays the psychological and moral conflicts of Guido, a man among men (and women). The two levels are developed before us side by side, each sustained by three different aspects of the activity of thought: memory (centered above all — in the manner of Joyce and Proust — on childhood subjects), dreams (generally aroused by the oppressive influence of others), reverie (visualization, as a rule, of desires or of his wandering in search of an inspiration).

In putting across these two different levels of the film and in having it supported now by memory, now by dreams, now by reverie, Fellini has never abandoned himself to the geometrical and somewhat abstract digressions of Resnais in *Marienbad*, nor to that dreamy, twilight atmosphere so dear to much of German expressionism. Instead, he has deliberately kept to a type of narration where everything arises naturally before the audience, with a clarity not threatened even by the rich exuberance of the photography or the scintillating variety of the secondary details. He has put the protagonist at the center of the action, has defined his state of mind, has explained, step by step, his development and the modes of this development, and then has asked the audience not to solve a riddle, but to abandon themselves to the emotive, lyrical, dramatic sensation which the film at every moment suggests to him so richly. Thus he resolutely turns his back on the Pirandellian philosophy (after *Six Characters in Search of an Author* it would have been easy to toy with an "Author in Search of Characters"), and only asks the gentlest, sincerest, and most human poetry to give his voice such limpid clarity that all may hear and understand.

The style, which can only be compared to the most accomplished moments of *La Strada* for a certain lyrical quality they show, is far superior to *La dolce vita* for maturity of expression, visual richness, firmness of rhythm, and linguistic and technical skill. Consider, for example, the setting of the action, that spa town with its Liberty-style hotels, which could be Aix-en-Provence fifty years ago, if we did not know that it is all invented ("Because," Fellini has said, "I didn't want to fall into the realist trap: I needed accuracy but the accuracy of dreams"). Consider those provincial cafés, those little concerts with *fin de siècle* music listened to by a colorful army of holiday-seekers, that rhythmical alternation of the cures, in an atmosphere now of ballet, now of a witches' Sabbath, among the hot-spring vapors, the waters, and the baths ("a kind of valley of Jehoshaphat," to quote Fellini again, "with a humanity of white phantoms, with the time spelled out by schedules — a limbo where everybody meets again, where it is possible to gaze at the images and faces of the past"). Consider again the meeting with a Cardinal who should give Guido, not altogether forgetful of a certain religious upbringing, useful advice on the way to follow. It takes place at the baths, amid steam and white sheets, in an atmosphere halfway between a Roman trireme and a convent and, notwithstanding the strangeness of the place and the apparent irreverence of the situation, is sustained by an almost mystical respect created by the hieratic rhythm of the solemn Latin quotations the very old and ascetic Prince of the Church pronounces to Guido in response to his opening: "Your Eminence, I'm not happy!"

And the memories? The familar brightness of those whitewashed walls of the childhood home (which will later welcome the picturesque reverie of the harem where, at last, all Guido's women will live at peace together), and the sickly whiteness of those boarding-school walls where, amid dark benches, dark confessionals and dark silhouettes of very severe priests, obsessed with the idea of the sinfulness of the flesh, little Guido will see instilled in him forever the antinomy between the devil-woman and the Virgin-mother, peculiar to a certain type of Catholic education.

Every scene, every sequence, has its own dramatic function, its own emotional value, its own exact pictorial importance sustained and focused by the steady perfection of every subsidiary element, from the photography (translucent and deliberately too white in certain initial reveries, shiningly romantic even in the most sombre parts, horrifying in the dreams), to the music, often based on well-known tunes and frequently used to introduce a precise atmosphere (for example, the lullaby for the chidhood scenes) or a character or situation of a definitely ironical turn (*The Dance of the Hours* for a highbrow, *Gigolette* for the empty-headed mistress, *The Ride of the Valkyrie* for the witches' Sabbath in the hot-spring baths and, later, for the revolt of the women in the harem).

And the final sequence, with all the characters in Guido's life, now dressed in white, parading affectionately around him, at last at peace with them, at last at peace with himself? The symbolism, which in other moments may falter, here transcends reality and attains to the most poignant poetry, in the most inspired and accomplished manner.

Federico Fellini

I VITELLONI

Alberto Sordi, Franco Interlenghi, Leo-
nora Ruffo, Franco Fabrizi, Leopoldo
Trieste, Lida Baarova, Paola Borboni,
Enrico Viarisio, Carlo Romano, Riccardo Fellini (Peg Film - Cité Film, 1953).

**I Vitelloni: provincial life poeticized. The first of Fellini's great ballads
on the Italian bourgeoisie and contemporary life. In a vein, at the
beginning, half-way between comedy and caricature.**

Federico Fellini

LA STRADA

Antony Quinn, Giulietta Masina, Rı-
chard Baseheart (Ponti-De Laurentiis,
1954).

La Strada is a moment of reflection, a pause for him to collect his
thoughts. It seems like a film out of its time. It has in it a noble
poetry and deeply serious ideas. Its photographic language is almost
rarefied, disdaining the precious in order to aim at the essential; but it
always achieves the warmth of an exquisite painting.

Federico Fellini

IL BIDONE

Broderick Crawford, Giulietta Masina,
Richard Baseheart, Franco Fabrizi (Titanus, 1955).

Federico Fellini

LE NOTTI DI CABIRIA
THE NIGHTS OF CABIRIA

Giulietta Masina, François Perier, Franca Marzi, Dorian Gray, Amedeo Nazzari (Dino De Laurentiis Cinemat., '56).

The Nights of Cabiria and Il Bidone prepare the way for La Dolce Vita. They are details, studied at closer range, in anticipation of the great fresco.

101

In the fresco of La Dolce Vita, there are all the contradictory aspects of the world of today. Expressed by Fellini with a vehemence in the choral groupings which deliberately ignores all cinema narrative conventions and with a poetry springing from the contrast, the shadows, and the horrors, in the manner of Baudelaire.

Federico Fellini

LA DOLCE VITA

Marcello Mastroianni, Anita Ekberg, Anouk Aimée, Luise Rainer, Lex Barker, Yvonne Fourneaux, Annibale Ninchi, Magali Noël (Riama Film, 1960).

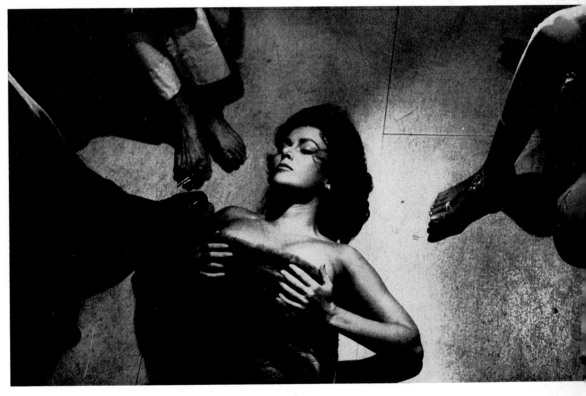

La Dolce Vita has a protagonist, but the chorus is the real hero.
A chorus which Fellini presents very freely in an original way, with a
photography too that is altogether untraditional.

Federico Fellini

LA DOLCE VITA

Marcello Mastroianni, Anita Ekberg,
Anouk Aimée, Luise Rainer, Lex Barker, Yvonne Fourneaux, Annibale Ninchi, Magali, Noël (Riama Film, 1960).

105

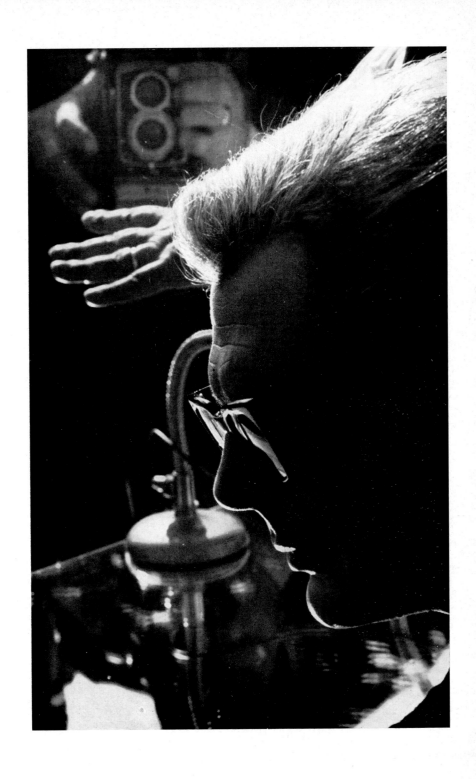

Federico Fellini

BOCCACCIO '70 (Le tentazioni del Dr. Antonio) - (Dr. Antonio's Temptations)

Anita Ekberg, Peppino De Filippo (Concordia Cinemat. - Cineriz - Francinex Gray Film, 1961).

8½

Marcello Mastroianni, Claudia Cardinale, Anouk Aimèe, Sandra Milo, Rossella Falk, Barbara Steele, Guido Alberti, Madeleine Lebeau, Jean Rougeul, Caterina Boratto (Cineriz, 1963).

After the lighthearted and debatable pause of Boccaccio '70, we have the great literary composition of 8½.

Federico Fellini

8½

Marcello Mastroianni, Claudia Cardinale, Anouk Aimèe, Sandra Milo, Rossella Falk, Barbara Steele, Guido Alberti, Madeleine Lebeau, Jean Rougeul, Caterina Boratto (Cineriz, 1963).

In 8½ there is Proust, Joyce, there is Pirandello: there is " la recherche du temps perdu " in order to rediscover ourselves and the reasons for living among other people.

Federico Fellini

8½

Marcello Mastroianni, Claudia Cardinale, Anouk Aimèe, Sandra Milo, Rossella Falk, Barbara Steele, Guido Alberti, Madeleine Lebeau, Jean Rougeul, Caterina Boratto (Cineriz, 1963).

In « 8½ » there is also the most exquisite invention the Italian cinema has ever given on the visual plane: a language which resorts to all the exuberant excesses of a baroque painting, all the arts of cinematographic technique, every possible abstraction, to create an atmosphere of visual hallucination able to express reality and fantasy, dreams and memories at the same time: with a balance that never fails.

After the panorama of La Dolce Vita and the revelatory drama of 8½, Fellini strikes a new key in Juliet of the Spirits a psychoanalytic approach to a human situation involving the various complexities of our era. The film has an obvious surrealistic inspiration and a rich play of fantasy and color, often transforming details into a baroque fantasmagoria that detracts from the unity of the work.

Federico Fellini

GIULIETTA DEGLI SPIRITI
JULIET OF THE SPIRITS

Giulietta Masina, Sandra Milo, Silva Koscina, Mario Pisu, Valentina Cortese, Elena Fondra, Silvana Jachino, Caterina Boratto, Luisa Della Noce, Lou Gilbert.

PIETRO GERMI

Born in Colombo (Liguria) on September 14, 1914.

Principal films:

Il testimone; Gioventù perduta; In nome della legge; Il cammino della speranza; La città si difende; Il brigante di Tacca del Lupo; La presidentessa; Gelosia; L'uomo di paglia; Un maledetto imbroglio; Divorzio all'Italiana; Sedotta e abbandonata; Signore e signori.

In recent years Pietro Germi has been giving increasing precision to his themes and his language, with a particularly careful study of everyday events, not exclusively along realistic lines, but examined also from inside, in a mood which at certain moments could actually be defined as romantic.

After the strictly literary, but dry and nervous experiment of *Gelosia* (*Jealousy*), in *L'uomo di paglia* (*Man of Straw*) and *Il ferroviere* we have him attempting a study of middle-class morals which, particularly in the former, almost seemed to belong to a certain cultural tradition of the French cinema, but which also showed he had a strong, determined personality, ready to reveal the most typical sides of the Italian character with minute analysis, sturdy accuracy, and at the same time passionate warmth. He bends his language to a formal perfection, a visual splendor, and a richness of photography which, however, are never ends in themselves, considering how faithful is their adherence to the themes that are enacted.

Sometimes he has been censured for an excessive warmth, a want of proportion, a too evident predilection for the passionate side, but these criticisms, even though partly justified, do not diminish the value or the austerity of Germi's films. Indeed, recently, in *Divorce Italian Style*, he has not only succeeded in getting rid of these defects, but has triumphantly overcome them all, initiating with authority and skill a new genre in our cinema, hitherto almost exclusively reserved to light authors: the comedy of manners.

In fact, the characters, the Sicilian landscape sur-

rounding them, the provincial habits, the Southern (nay, island) mentality, are all caricatured in accents pitched one, or even two, notes above reality, but the point they start out from is authentic, the picture they sketch, though distorted by satire, is realistic in origin and, even when it is not true, is truthlike, so that the results are delightful. Of course, their success was guaranteed in advance by a story which seems lifted bodily from a delightful satirical novel that provides the richness of the themes, the warm precision of the characters, and the sound narrative structure. But the director makes use of all the happiest tricks of the cinema to bring to life a film in which the gay rhythm never fails, the parody never flags (always rich in invention, ironical suggestions, and amusing asides), and the artful attacks hidden between the folds of the irony never for an instant slacken their fire.

There is, however, less aesthetic balance, and even a disconcerting wandering between polemics and open farce, in *Seduced and Abandoned*, an often violent parody on those articles of our law which, when marriage intervenes, authorize the release from prison of a person guilty of the crimes of abduction and corruption of a minor.

This time the cast, their characters, and frequently even their physical appearance, are immersed in an atmosphere reminiscent of George Grosz, permeated only by harshness and, at times, by such a pitiless ferocity that Germi appears to show chiefly antipathy and contempt towards them, and never a grain of pity. If this antipathy has enabled the director to create figures all of a piece, carefully analysed in their every particular, it has also led him to depart from the limits of ordinary reality to such a degree that each character often appears more like a mask than like a person, and the story, instead of succeeding as a satirical comedy, oversteps even the limits of farce into the world of grotesquerie, doubtful and ambiguous, charged with sullen, gloomy resentment.

The style, too, obeys this formula: vehement, jerky, sometimes downright stormy, it nevertheless often admits contradictory elements such as certain dreams and reveries of a grimly baroque taste in contrast to the peasant flavor the story would like to preserve, and certain abrupt transitions which, because they take too many liberties with grammar, harm the onward flow of the story and seem a bit like the old cinema.

To this it should be added that the action, notwithstanding the intentional frenzy of its narrative rhythm, is here and there a little static and prolix and, especially in the second half, it contains so many dramatic elements, so dwelt on, so diffuse, so unessential, as to harm the balance of the film and its clarity.

Still, one is bound to recognize that the vitality of some figures is at times such as to recall, in certain moments, certain Sicilian sketches of Pirandello (the story, once again, is set in Sicily), and that the whirl of events, humorous and semidramatic by turns, in which they find themselves, makes for real, solid entertainment, for the sparkling gaiety of some of his funny inventions and, conversely, for the ease with which he is able to balance them with harsher and more serious scenes.

And these merits are due to a director who, even when he makes mistakes, be they only through excess, never betrays the laws of spectacle.

A page of realism and literature together, this is Jealousy. The blacks and whites of Sicily again find in Germi an artist at once austere and inspired.

Pietro Germi

GELOSIA - JEALOUSY

Marisa Belli, Erno Crisa, Liliana Geraci, Vincenzo Musolino, Paola Borboni (Excelsa Film, 1953).

Realist and romantic at the same time, Germi, in Man of Straw, faces everyday themes with a passionate warmth at times even excessive, but always with a vigorous form which, with him, springs spontaneously from the humble circles the action takes place in.

Pietro Germi

L'UOMO DI PAGLIA - MAN OF STRAW

Pietro Germi, Luisa Della Noce, Saro Urzì, Franca Bettoja, Edoardo Nevola (Lux - Vides, 1957).

Pietro Germi

UN MALEDETTO IMBROGLIO
A CURSED TANGLE

Pietro Germi, Claudia Cardinale, Franco Fabrizi, Cristina Gajoni, Claudio Gora, Saro Urzì, Peppino de Martino (Riama Cinematografia, 1959).

In A Cursed Tangle, Germi transforms a polished literary text (Quer pasticciaccio brutto de via Merulana, by Carlo Emilio Gadda) into a skillful detective film, supported by solid logic and enlivened by neat, foursquare characters. But his ability in humorous vein was revealed by Divorce Italian Style, which, notwithstanding its polemical purpose, develops into one of the most successful, delightfully amusing comedies of manners in the Italian cinema, sustained throughout by a language lavish with all the severest attributes of style.

Pietro Germi

DIVORZIO ALL'ITALIANA
DIVORCE ITALIAN STYLE

Marcello Mastroianni, Daniela Rocca,
Stefania Sandrelli, Leopoldo Trieste,
Odoardo Spadaro (Lux-Vides, 1961).

Pietro Germi

DIVORZIO ALL'ITALIANA
DIVORCE ITALIAN STYLE

Marcello Mastroianni, Daniela Rocca,
Stefania Sandrelli, Leopoldo Trieste,
Odoardo Spadaro (Lux-Vides, 1961).

Seduced and Abandoned is a repetition of Divorce Italian Style. Here polemical harshness prevails over the comedy, savage caricature over the humor, and the story, packed with minor episodes, poorly balanced and not very harmonious, in spite of its frankly presented characters, is not fully convincing. And this notwithstanding its Sicilian setting teeming not only with local color, but also with the precise delineation of customs.

Pietro Germi

SEDOTTA E ABBANDONATA
SEDUCED AND ABANDONED

Stefania Sandrelli, Saro Urzì, Aldo Puglisi, Nando Buzzanca, Leopoldo Trieste (Vides Film, 1964).

119

ALBERTO LATTUADA

Born in Milan on November 13, 1914.

Principal films:

Giacomo l'Idealista; La freccia nel fianco; Il bandito; Il delitto di Giovanni Episcopo; Senza pietà; Il mulino del Po; Luci del varietà; Anna; Il cappotto; L'amore in città (an episode); La Lupa; La spiaggia; Guendalina; I dolci inganni; Lettere di una novizia; L'imprevisto; Il mafioso; La steppa; Controsesso (an episode); Mandragola.

Alberto Lattuada, who in the immediate postwar period had presented the solemn chorale of *The Mill on the Po*, in recent years has often returned to literary sources, as if his culture and austere photography were better served by learned founts of inspiration.

He followed *La Lupa (The She-Wolf)*, at once realistic and precious, drawn from Verga's short story, with (1957) the pleasant sentimental scherzo *Guendalina* — an accurate and precise, felicitous and amusing portrait of teenage love affairs. He then went for inspiration to some tales of Pushkin, giving us, in *Tempest*, a colorful picture of the eighteenth-century Russia of Catherine the Great. Great care is taken over the minor as well as the leading characters, and the composition of every picture is studied with keen pictorial sense.

Later (1960) Lattuada returned to the problem of adolescence, already so charmingly dealt with in *Guendalina*, and, in *Dolci inganni (Sweet Deceptions)*, he tells with inspired accuracy the story of a day in the life of a girl of seventeen, a day of particular importance, seeing that it marks the passing of childhood innocence into the search for, and, later, the discovery of love.

The psychological progression of this day is followed with particular attention and with a freshness in the descriptions which, if in certain marginal episodes they seem a little facile or literary, are almost always successful when they serve to clarify the protagonist's states of mind, her somewhat morbid anxiety, her searching, her hesitations, her uncertainty.

Going from Pushkin to Piovene, in *Lettere di una novizia (The Novice)* Lattuada makes an attempt, following a famous literary text, at psychological introspection, but with results which are somewhat uneven. But later on he will achieve better results in *La steppa (The Steppe)*, based on a story by Anton Chekhov who, in order to describe in quasi-symbolical vein a boy's passing from childhood to adolescence, pictured him making a journey across the Steppes with his mother, from the village where he was born to the town where he was going to live.

Lattuada has transferred the story from Russia to Yugoslavia, perhaps in order to find certain *fin de siècle* atmospheres and settings more untouched, and, although his narrative rhythm is not always lively enough, he has succeeded in recreating Chekhov's mood with a deliberately polished, literary language. He is particularly successful in certain group scenes, in drawing the painful resignation of minor figures, and in the inner study of the steady development of the boy's character, displaying a technical skill which, especially where it sustains the action with an appropriately sonorous musical counterpoint, achieves the dignity of style.

This technique and style will later, in *L'imprevisto (Unexpected)* and in *Il mafioso (Mafioso)*, enable Lattuada to achieve some particularly powerful results, thanks to that inner austerity which (a proof of his now secure mastery of the cinema) will make it ever easier for him to attain mature levels: in *Unexpected*, a detective story told with the sureness of a master hand; and in *Mafioso*, a psychological study which, though belonging to the genre of satirical comedy, goes beyond it in the vigor of its polemics which cannot but give everyone serious food for thought.

Alberto Lattuada

LA LUPA - THE SHE-WOLF

Kerima, May Britt, Ettore Manni, Giovanna Ralli, Mario Passante, Ignazio Balsamo (Ponti-De Laurentiis, 1952).

Open to the suggestions of a varied culture and to widely differing types of spectacle, Lattuada knows how to follow the satirical report on the summer relaxations of the rich bourgeoisie (The Beach) with a charming description of an encounter between two adolescents (Guendalina), even in the less important sequences revealing an elegant and gifted language.

Alberto Lattuada

GUENDALINA

Jacqueline Sassard, Raffaele Mattioli, Raf Vallone, Sylva Koscina, Leda Gloria (Carlo Ponti Cinematografica, 1957).

LA SPIAGGIA - THE BEACH

Martine Carol, Raf Vallone, Mario Carotenuto, Clelia Matania, Rosy Mazzacurati, Carlo Romano (Titanus, 1953).

Tempest is evidence of his literary needs: it is, in fact, a scholarly rereading of Pushkin, with a photography which, in the wake of The Mill on the Po, shows us a Lattuada more alive to the composition of the pictures and to the harmony and complexity of the chromatic values.

Alberto Lattuada

LA TEMPESTA - TEMPEST

Silvana Mangano, Geoffrey Horne, Van Heflin, Viveca Lindfors, Vittorio Gassman, Helmut Dantine, Guido Celano, Aldo Silvani, Claudio Gora (Dino De Laurentiis Cinematografica-Bosnia Film, 1958).

Alberto Lattuada
I DOLCI INGANNI - SWEET DECEPTIONS
Catherine Spaak, Christian Marquand,
Jean Sorel, Claudio Gora, Patrizia Bini,
Milly (Titanus - Laetitia Film - Les
Films Marceau - Cocinor, 1960).

LETTERE DI UNA NOVIZIA - THE NOVICE
Pascal Petit, Jean Paul Belmondo, Mas-
simo Girotti, Lilla Brignone, Elsa Vaz-
zoler, Hella Petri (Euro International
Film - Les Films Modernes - Les Films
Agiman, 1960).

In Sweet Deceptions, we are back in the world of Guendalina, but
from the point of view of a full-grown adolescent girl making her
first venture into the world of love. A psychological portrait sensitively
developed on the razor's edge of a complicated problem, Sweet Deceptions is stylistically richer and warmer than The Novice, a literary
transcription in which Lattuada does not succeed in giving the full
measure of his talent.

126

Alberto Lattuada

L'IMPREVISTO - UNEXPECTED

Anouk Aimée, Tomas Milian, Raymond Pellegrin, Jacques Morel (Documento Film - Orsay Film, 1961).

After psychology, the detective film: Unexpected, impeccably constructed, with clear-cut, well-defined characters. It is a little artificial and mechanical, of course, but these are defects inherent in the genre. Harsher, in spite of its rifts of humor, is Mafioso, a rigorous, controversial work, farcical only on the surface, perhaps not always very clear in its psychological motivation, but most effective in its narrative construction.

128

Alberto Lattuada

Il mafioso - Mafioso

Alberto Sordi, Norma Bengell, Cinzia Bruno, Katiuscia Piretti (Antonio Cervi, 1962).

Alberto Lattuada

LA STEPPA - THE STEPPE

Daniele Spallone, Marina Vlady, Charles Vanel, Cristina Gajoni, Pablo Vuijsic (Zebra Film - Aera Film, 1962).

Another film from a literary text: The Steppe, by Chekhov. Here Lattuada achieves the impalpable transparency of Chekhov's situations, exactly reproducing all their symbols and all the human warmth they poetically hide, with a highly gifted technique in every detail.

CARLO LIZZANI

Born in Rome on April 3, 1922.

Principal films:

Acktung banditi; Ai margini della metropoli; Amore in città (an episode); Cronache di poveri amanti; La muraglia cinese; Il gobbo; L'oro di Roma; Il processo di Verona; Vita agra; Celestina; Amori pericolosi; La guerra segreta; Thrilling (an episode); Delitto di lusso.

Like De Santis, Carlo Lizzani has a political ax to grind, but he pays more attention to the needs of cinematographic language: whether he goes to a novel for inspiration, as in *Cronache di poveri amanti* (*True Stories of Poor Lovers*), or confronts the most burning themes of contemporary life, as in *Oro di Roma* (*Rome's Gold*) or *Il gobbo* (*The Hunchback of Rome*), he always displays assured and proven craftsmanship.

In *Cronache di poveri amanti* this craftsmanship rises to the most passionate lyricism, charged with indignation and bitter moods. In *Oro di Roma* he perhaps lets himself be checked by an austerity of expression which borders on coldness. In *Il gobbo*, taking over the soundest themes of the American detective film, he initiates an adventure genre in our cinema which bases its main lines on real events, but raises them to the level of grand adventure, at the same time attempting a character study developed in a hard, merciless, singularly convincing way, from which a character results, in some respects seeming to be based on the Hollywood gangster model, but in fact always having its own well-marked originality. This is due not only to the different milieu in which the character acts (Rome during and immediately after the war — the cruelties, the black market, the crime of those years when the law was en-

forced only with difficulty), but also and above all to the critical attitude with which it is described in an atmosphere of implicit polemical restraint.

Lizzani has dealt with this study, and also the setting which acts as its background, with a harsh, and violent, but also severe, and clear-cut language, carefully drawing the most complex psychological schemes and successfully creating the most dramatic atmospheres on the lines (as regards photography and narrative rhythm) of the best American gangster films. This "imitation" has not, however, prevented him from seeing men and things, backgrounds and settings, according to the severest lessons of the Italian neorealist school, enriched by a mature mastery of all the rules of cinematographic spectacle.

These rules, applied now not to crime reports but to recent history, enable Lizzani, in *The Verona Trial*, to achieve an exemplary dramatic tension, drawing from real-life people and their universally known adventures the elements for a story made to conquer the hearts of the most critical cinema audiences, with a technique which, without despising any of the successful advances of the American cinema, adapts them to the needs of our severest representationalism.

News reports and history are the themes nearest to Lizzani's heart, since they enable him to carry the neorealist lesson as far as the most serious achievements of the spectacular cinema of today — as in True Stories of Poor Lovers, where literature and the drama are fused into the perfect reconstruction of an epoch, an outlook, and a setting.

Carlo Lizzani

CRONACHE DI POVERI AMANTI
TRUE STORIES OF POOR LOVERS

Anna Maria Ferrero, Cosetta Greco, Antonella Lualdi, Marcello Mastroianni, Wanda Capodaglio (Cooperativa Spettatori Produttori Cinematografici, 1953).

Carlo Lizzani

Il gobbo - The hunchback of rome

Gerard Blain, Anna Maria Ferrero, Bernard Blier, Ivo Garrani, Pier Paolo Pasolini (Dino De Laurentiis Cinematografica, 1960).

Rome's Gold, a film devoted to the German occupation of Rome, is particularly lively and passionate in several places. The Hunchback of Rome is a gangster film in Italian style, the photography of which is in the tradition of neorealism at its best.

Carlo Lizzani

L'ORO DI ROMA - ROME'S GOLD

Anna Maria Ferrero, Gérard Blain, Jean
Sorel, Filippo Scelzo, Paola Borboni,
Andrea Checchi (Sancro Film - Ager
Film - Cirac - Rotfield - Contact Org.,
1961).

Carlo Lizzani

IL PROCESSO DI VERONA - THE VERONA TRIAL

Silvana Mangano, Frank Wolf, Vivi Gioi,
François Prévost, Salvo Randone, Clau-
dio Gora, Filippo Scelzo, Giorgio De
Lullo, Ivo Garrani, Carlo D'Angelo
(Duilio Cinematografica S.p.A. - Orsay
Film, 1962).

In The Verona Trial, history becomes crime reporting: dry, dramatic,
delirious, with pitiless rigor and a rare intensity of emotional climates.
With the reconstruction of a period and a setting (the winter of 1944,
occupied Italy, Verona), it is often quite exemplary in its imagery.

MARIO MONICELLI

Born in Viareggio on May 16, 1915.

Principal films:

Un eroe dei nostri tempi; Padri e figli; I soliti ignoti; La grande guerra; Risate di gioia; Boccaccio '70 (an episode); I compagni; Casanova '70; La bugiarda; I Complessi (an episode); L'Armata Brancaleone.

Mario Monicelli is a director who, with his latest films, has definitely been acquiring a prominent place in our cinema. With *I soliti ignoti (The Big Deal on Madonna Street)* he had taken his place among our best creators of comedy with an ease, a wealth of fantasy, a fire and versatility which few could equal in this field. All the more so because, though the film attempted comic themes at length and in the tradition of the Italian comedy, it succeeded in ennobling them with a rather unusual dignity, even in the caricature, and with a verve which never failed, notwithstanding the complexity of an action producing surprises at every step, as if sustained by an inexhaustible energy. Moreover, instead of becoming slack, considering the easy nature of the themes, the style always aimed at a taut severity and a high standard of taste in the photography.

The same style and taste, wedded to a more restrained and quieter humorous vein, were to be hugely successful — almost clamorously so — in *The Great War*, which was not just the amusing story of two cowardly soldiers, but rather a complete portrait of the most vivid pages and most heroic moments of the 1914-18 war, not in epic style, but true and sincere all the same, with a photography relying for its atmosphere on black and white pictures cleverly imitating the soft tones of the old photographs of the time, without errors of taste or founderings of any kind.

There is the same fine photography, but less dramatic interest, in *The Organizer*, made by Monicelli immediately after the short and not very convincing episode he contributed to *Boccaccio '70* (" Renzo and Luciana "). Here the study of the first labor struggles in *fin de siècle* Turin becomes chiefly a reconstruction of the setting, with a search for the tunes typical of a period and an almost archaelogical attention to predominating details. The characters are a little artificial and, when they do get across, they do so only for a certain external argumentative violence. However, the film is noble and severe, and its language is a confirmation of the best talents of a director whose photography is outstanding.

Monicelli's humor, with The Big Deal on Madonna Street, has given to the Italian cinema some of the freshest and liveliest sequences of Italian comedy.

Mario Monicelli

I SOLITI IGNOTI
THE BIG DEAL ON MADONNA STREET

Vittorio Gassman, Renato Salvatori, Rossana Rory, Carla Gravina, Claudia Cardinale, Carlo Pisacane, Tiberio Murgia, Memmo Carotenuto, Marcello Mastroianni, Totò (Lux Film - Vides, 1958).

139

Mario Monicelli

La grande guerra - The great war

Alberto Sordi, Vittorio Gassman, Bernard Blier, Nicola Arigliano, Geronimo Meynier, Elsa Vazzoler, Tiberio Murgia, Livio Lorenzon, Ferruccio Amendola, Mario Valdemarin, Silvana Mangano, (Dino De Laurentiis Cinemat., 1959).

Monicelli's humor blends with sincere, human themes in The Great War, and, as regards the photography, it rises to the dignity of an environment evoked with inspired, scholarly style, made up of minute details, filtered through the pictorial records of an epoch — Italy 1915-18.

Mario Monicelli

Boccaccio '70 (Renzo e Luciana)
(Renzo and Luciana)

Marisa Solinas, Germano Giglioli (Concordia Cinemat. - Cineriz - Francinex Gray Film, 1961).

I compagni - The organizer

Marcello Mastroianni, Renato Salvatori, Annie Girardot, Bernard Blier, Gabriella Giorgelli, François Périer, Folco Lulli, Vittorio Sanipoli (Lux-Vides, '63).

The same evocative skill in The Organizer, where Turin at the beginning of the century lives again in pictorial clarity, in an atmosphere which is entirely faithful on the human and social level also.

143

Mario Monicelli

I COMPAGNI - THE ORGANIZER

Marcello Mastroianni, Renato Salvatori, Annie Girardot, Bernard Blier, Gabriella Giorgelli, François Périer, Folco Lulli, Vittorio Sanipoli (Lux-Vides, '63).

The conversations, customs, and habits seem to have been reconstructed here with the patience of a researcher; they have the savor of authentic utensils unearthed in an antique shop. And the human dramas they enshrine have the authentic note of memories handed down by word of mouth.

ANTONIO PIETRANGELI

Born in Rome on January 19, 1919.

Principal films:

Il sole negli occhi; Lo scapolo; Nata di marzo; Adua e le compagne; Fantasmi a Roma; La Parmigiana; La visita; Il magnifico cornuto.

Antonio Pietrangeli is a director who for years has come under the influence of various widely differing inspirations. First, in *Il sole negli occhi* (*Sun in the Eyes*), he attempts with a certain freshness a serio-comic sketch of life, or rather popular life, in Rome; then, in *Lo scapolo* (*The Bachelor*), he indulges in easy-going comedy in deference to the custom of the day. But if *Souvenir d'Italie* represents a too easy concession to the conventional fashion of episode films, in *Nata di marzo* (*March's Child*), which confronts the theme of incompatibility in marriage, he resurrects a comic vein rather unusual in our cinema, creating characters, situations, and states of mind which may be considered among the liveliest to appear on our screens lately.

Thus the occasion, as well as a certain social interest never quite given up, lead him in *Adua e le compagne* (*Adua and Her Companions*) to deal (firmly and sympathetically and, of course, always with a live touch of humor) with the problem of the prostitutes left homeless by the Merlin Law. At times he achieves some very human effects, with a solid, precise language.

In *Fantasmi a Roma* this language will even attempt the most colorful paths of fantasy, composing a portrait of patrician Rome, picturesquely animated by clouds of ghosts and accompanied by the most delightfully gay farcical touches. But, notwithstanding an uncommon care over the narrative, his second to last film, *La parmigiana* (*The Girl from Parma*), on the life and misadventures of a prostitute, is not altogether successful. Still, it does give a clear portrait of a woman, colorful, thorough, and very curious, and a description of provincial circles which, for its savor and its subtle controversial atmosphere, seems to be inspired by the best literary tradition of the genre.

Equally debatable, at least as regards the directing, is his latest film, *La visita* (*The Visit*), devoted in bitter irony to two lonely hearts, a country spinster and a town bachelor, who meet as result of a matrimonial advertisement, and, after a whole day spent together, reveal to each other those differences of character which will take them back to their desolate loneliness.

Although the directing is rather ordinary and the photography shows little brilliance, the story has the undeniable merit of presenting two characters who are really fully drawn. It also traces with steady hand the development of these two characters as they gradually explain themselves to each other, and gives a fairly complete picture of a clash between different habits, opposite aspirations, and outlooks which for several reasons are foreign to each other. And though it is largely conceived in comic, if not downright farcical vein, it is often streaked with melancholy reflections. The style is economical to the point of austerity.

Pietrangeli won widespread acclaim for his most recent film, *The Magnificent Cuckold*, in which he draws freely but skillfully upon the celebrated farce by Crommelynck. Here once again he gives us a spicy portrait of provincial Italian life, offset in this case by all the anguish of love and, above all, jealousy, recalling a comedy of manners in its vitality, flavor, and zestful humor. Although it continually threatens to overstep the boundaries of farce, it succeeds in keeping them. Even when it becomes rowdy and broad, its tone remains light and it is never heavyhanded.

Antonio Pietrangeli

IL SOLE NEGLI OCCHI - SUN IN THE EYES

Gabriele Ferzetti, Irene Galter, Paolo Stoppa (Titanus - Film Costellazione, 1953)

Antonio Pietrangeli

NATA DI MARZO - MARCH'S CHILD

Jacqueline Sassard, Gabriele Ferzetti, Mario Valdemarin, Tina De Mola (P. Cinematografica - Film Marceu, 1957).

A quarrel between husband and wife carried on with the free and easy charm of a French comedy: March's Child. A portrait almost from life of a group of prostitutes left homeless after the Merlin Law: Adua and Her Companions. Here the warmth of an understanding humanity is salted with an irony rarely guilty of bad taste.

Antonio Pietrangeli

ADUA E LE COMPAGNE
ADUA AND HER COMPANIONS

Simone Signoret, Sandra Milo, Emmanuelle Riva, Marcello Mastroianni, Gina Rovere, Ivo Garrani, Gianrico Tedeschi (Zebra Film, 1960).

149

A fable in color lived on the roofs of the Eternal City: Ghosts in Rome.
It is a "scherzo" but it enables Pietrangeli to match color technique
with refined taste and warm inspiration.

Antonio Pietrangeli

FANTASMI A ROMA - GHOST'S IN ROME

Marcello Mastroianni, Belinda Lee,
Sandra Milo, Edoardo De Filippo,
Claudio Gora, Tino Buazzelli, Franca
Marzi, Ida Galli, Vittorio Gassman
(Lux - Vides - Galatea, 1960).

Antonio Pietrangeli

LA PARMIGIANA - THE GIRL FROM PARMA

Catherine Spaak, Nino Manfredi, Didi
Perego, Lando Buzzanca, Vanni De Maigret, Salvo Randone, Rosalia Maggio,
Umberto D'Orsi, Mario Brega (Documento Film, 1963).

LA VISITA - THE VISIT

Sandra Milo, François Périer, Mario
Adorf, Angela Minervini, Gastone Moschin (Zebra Film, 1964).

The Girl from Parma draws a delightful portrait of provincial life;
from the narrative point of view, however, it reveals weak points which
the psychology of the characters, often uncertain enough in itself, is
not able to redeem. The characters are more concrete in The Visit, a
film in which Pietrangeli seems to have taken little trouble over the
style, but which, on the psychological level, gives him the opportunity
to draw, with somewhat bitter irony a highly colored contrast in a
pleasantly rural village setting.

GIANNI PUCCINI

Born in Milan on November 9, 1914.

Principal films:

Parola di ladro; Carmela è una bambola; Il nemico di mia moglie; Il carro armato dell'8 settembre; L'attico; Cuori infranti (an episode).

After collaborating in various films, Gianni Puccini made his debut as a director in his own right with *Il carro armato dell'8 settembre*, a modest film on the turbulent days of the armistice, seen from a point of view only in part realistic.

He then made *L'impiegato (The Employee)*. It was an attempt to introduce into our cinema that fanciful formula of dreams strictly linked to reality which had so much success in the American cinema, but he ended up a victim of his own tour de force, always vainly suspended between contradictions in style and irregularities in the narrative.

So, later on, in *L'attico*, although he had tried to give a finished portrait of a woman social climber who really started out from under the stairs and triumphantly reached the attic, he has let himself be led away by secondary figures and, instead of a compact, homogeneous story, with soundly contrived characters, he has constructed an uneven and not very harmonious tale, animated by types and eccentrics more like masks than real characters.

However, within its limits, the episode he directed in *Cuori infranti, Vissero contenti e felici* is more convincing — always halfway between caricature and paradox, but gracefully sustained by a delicate, light humor, without too many jarring notes, though, perhaps, here and there it is rather simple and naïve.

Gianni Puccini's The Attic is a page from contemporary Italian life. Irregularities in the narrative prevent it from being a finished work, but it presents a gallery of characters, alive and clearcut, all typical faces in the news of our time.

Gianni Puccini

L'ATTICO - THE ATTIC

Daniela Rocca, Walter Chiari, Tomas Milian, Philippe Leroy, Jean Jacques Delbo, Lilla Brignone, Mary Arden, Gino Pernice (Galatea S.p.A., 1962).

DINO RISI

Born in Milan on December 23, 1916.

Principal films:

Poveri ma belli; Il vedovo; Una vita difficile; Il sorpasso; I mostri; Il giovedì.

After an experiment with a low-budget film, *Poor But Beautiful*, told, moreover, with undeniable aplomb, Dino Risi brought himself to the critics' notice with *Il vedovo* (*The Window*), a film in which he succeeded with definite vigor in blending Anglo-Saxon macabre humor with the more openly farcical themes of Italian comedy. But more serious notice began to be taken of him after *Una vita difficile* (*A Hard Life*). In tracing the psychological portrait of an Italian caught between the war and the postwar period, this film managed to point out all the controversial topics of our time very clearly, while avoiding the temptation to turn the opportunities for comedy the story offered into material for easy laughs, giving them instead their precise significance in the story.

But his most significant and important work to date is the recently produced *The Easy Life*. Putting the accent on a typical character of our times, the cocksure braggart who is really a failure at bottom, he confronts themes and problems of Italian life in a vivid, lively way, alternating farce with satire, caricature with polemics. The cleverly constructed story is carried to a solution with limpid clarity, with never a single slackening in the rhythm, and in an atmosphere of carefree gaiety sharply concluded on a very painful, bitter note.

In *I mostri* (*The Monsters*), however, his attempt to draw a gallery of the more or less abnormal figures of our times in lively colors is only superficially successful, because the types chosen are rather vague. Some go no further than the joke, others stop short at the sketch, and all, in general, are put together with little sense of proportion, with a view to easy caricature. The last portrait is an exception: it is of a boxer in retirement, and has a genuine dramatic inwardness, a pathetic resonance, and, at times, a really exemplary photographic dignity.

The opposite defects, but with identical results, are found in *Il giovedì* (*Thursday*), Risi's latest film. It is the story of an unusual day which sees a father, five years after being separated from his wife, meet his eight-year-old son, now completely strange to him. In spite of its sincere human descriptions and delicate states of mind, the film never goes deeply into the clash between the two characters, simply giving flimsy examples of states of mind rather to be expected. Still, here and there, especially in its analysis of the boy's character, it does reach a certain emotional intensity.

Dino Risi

Poveri ma belli - Poor but beatiful

Marisa Allasio, Maurizio Arena, Renato Salvatori, Memmo Carotenuto, Alessandra Panaro, Mario Carotenuto, Lorella De Luca, Virgilio Riento (Titanus, 1956).

Dino Risi

UNA VITA DIFFICILE - A HARD LIFE

Alberto Sordi, Lea Massari, Franco Fabrizi, Lina Volonghi, Claudio Gora, Antonio Centa (Dino De Laurentiis Cinemat., 1961).

A Hard Life is the often sincere synopsis of the vicissitudes encountered by the average Italian man in the last twenty years, with descriptions that are at times felicitous. Of wider scope, although it does not generalize in any way, is The Easy Life, which, in describing a very topical figure, finds the exact measure of caricaturist comedy, and with a balance which, except for certain pasages, is able to remain on an exemplary level even in the most open moments of farce.

Dino Risi

IL SORPASSO - THE EASY LIFE

Vittorio Gassman, Catherine Spaak, Jean Louis Trintignant, Claudio Gora, Luciana Angiolillo, Linda Sini (Fair Film - Incei Film - Sancro Film, 1962).

Dino Risi

I MOSTRI - THE MONSTERS
Vittorio Gassman, Ugo Tognazzi, Marisa Merlini, Lando Buzzanca, Rica Dialine, Marino Masè, Michele Mercier (Titanus, 1963).

IL GIOVEDÌ - THURSDAY
Walter Chiari, Michele Mercier, Robertino, Gemelle Kessler (Dino De Laurentiis S.p.A. - Centerfilm S.p.A., 1964).

In The Monsters, the farce is more obvious and not more than a sketch, and it succeeds only at intervals on the level of external caricature and jokes. Of an opposite tone, but equally unresolved, is Thursday, a conflict between father and son drawn without much bite and along narrative lines without much originality.

FRANCESCO ROSI

Born in Naples on November 15, 1922.

Principal films:

La sfida; I magliari; Salvatore Giuliano; Le mani sulla città; Il momento della verità.

A vigorous, fighting, committed director, Francesco Rosi was an immediate success in the Italian cinema with a film set in Naples. *La sfida* (*The Challenge*), with brigandage and graft, love stories and rival factions, gave us a clear-cut portrait of a certain Neapolitan mentality, with a technique already so wise and wary as in many places to attain the vigor of style.

But this vigor, even more mature in *I magliari* (*The Hawkers*), was to be put to the service of a story — set in Germany among Italian emigrants — not always supported by an adequate inspiration or, even more important, by a precise, basic study of the characters, which are too often presented in a merely external way without solid human reflection.

The film, however, which was to set the seal on Rosi's cinematographic fortune was *Salvatore Giuliano*, a documentary on the life and death of the bandit of Montelepre. This film which, notwithstanding its dramatic plot, claims to be chiefly a documentary, is built up exclusively on the reports of the *Carabinieri*, the accounts of the special correspondents of the principal newspapers, and lastly, on the records of the Viterbo trial of Pisciotta and company. Personal interpretations are reduced to a minimum and (the existing ones are chiefly those put forward by certain journalistic inquiries) always kept within the limits of actual news reports. It may be objected that, with this method of telling the story, the director has not succeeded in creating a real character, or at least not one of those characters with a psychology all of a piece to which the cinema-novel has accustomed us. Or again that, while leaving much to be understood by the audience regarding the events concerned, it offers no " revelations " to answer the questions public opinion once asked itself about the " myth " and the end of Giuliano. But it must be admitted that this refusal to adopt conventional forms gives the whole film an atmosphere of concrete, actual reality so convincing that you forget the fictional nature of the " shots " and think the story is a documentary drawn from life.

It is a sensation which arouses emotions almost unbearably keen, so true to life are the sequences on Giuliano's death and funeral, the Viterbo trial, the slaughter at Portella delle Ginestre, and the manhunt in Montelepre. Here the director's language definitely rises to a dignity of style, using a photography which, while not forgetting a reliable pictorial tradition, tends to reduce it to the bare, concrete essentials in the manner of the best Italian neorealism.

In *Mani sulla città* (*Hands on the Town*) there is more polemics and less poetry. The very topical theme of building speculation has found in Rosi a passionate disputant, but certainly not an inspired narrator, notwithstanding some sequences of pure directing which, for their vehemence and burning zeal, have once more recommended his style to the respect of the critics. What impressed them, from many points of view, was the novelty of his attempt to give a completely unusual cinematographic dress to a peroration which often passes into tense drama.

In a different mood, but perhaps just as questionable, we have Rosi's most recent film *Il momento della verità* (*Moment of Truth*), which, in the spirit of the *cinéma-verité*, tells the life story of a bullfighter from his humble beginnings to his final glory and death in the bullring.

The rules of the *cinéma-verité* led Rosi to develop his theme with total objectivity, like a document but always a " reconstructed " document, a simulation of reality dramatized according to stylistic requirements. For this reason, the over all result is unconvincing. Its drama remains unconvincing precisely because the *cinéma-verité* admits no viewpoint. If it does not actually distort its characters, it at least deprives them of any psychological validity.

Beyond this his style is often contradictory, caught between its desire to be " factual " and, at the same time, insistently intellectualizing its theme.

Nonetheless, the film unquestionably has effective dramatic moments, particularly in its documentation of a bullfight in which we all but feel the heat and glare of the Spanish sun.

Francesco Rosi

LA SFIDA - THE CHALLENGE

Josè Suarez, Rosanna Schiaffino, Nino
Vingelli, Decimo Cristiani (Lux - Vides,
1957).

**The Challenge, by Francesco Rosi is a scorching picture of Neapolitan
life, pervaded by violent and dramatic indignation.**

163

Francesco Rosi

I MAGLIARI - THE HAWKERS

Alberto Sordi, Belinda Lee, Renato Salvatori, Nino Vingelli, Aldo Giuffré, Linda Vandal, Nino di Napoli, Aldo Landi (Titanus - Vides, 1959).

After the hard, clear portrait of a group of Italian emigrants — in The Hawkers — we have the severely realistic page of Salvatore Giuliano, a film which sets out to be a document — an objective document whose pictorial quality gives its scenes the most genuine air of authenticity, of a news report taken from life, through a realistic formula most effective on the screen.

Francesco Rosi

SALVATORE GIULIANO

Frank Wolf, Cicero Fernando, Salvo Randone, Sennuccio Benelli, Bruno Ukmar, Max Cartier (Lux - Vides - Galatea, 1961).

Francesco Rosi

LE MANI SULLA CITTÀ - HANDS ON THE TOWN

Rod Steiger, Salvo Randone, Guido Alberti (Galatea, 1963).

But Hands on the Town is polemics and not cinema. Even here, however, Rosi's style has the chance to sketch some unimpeachable sequences in his sympathetic reconstruction of an environment.

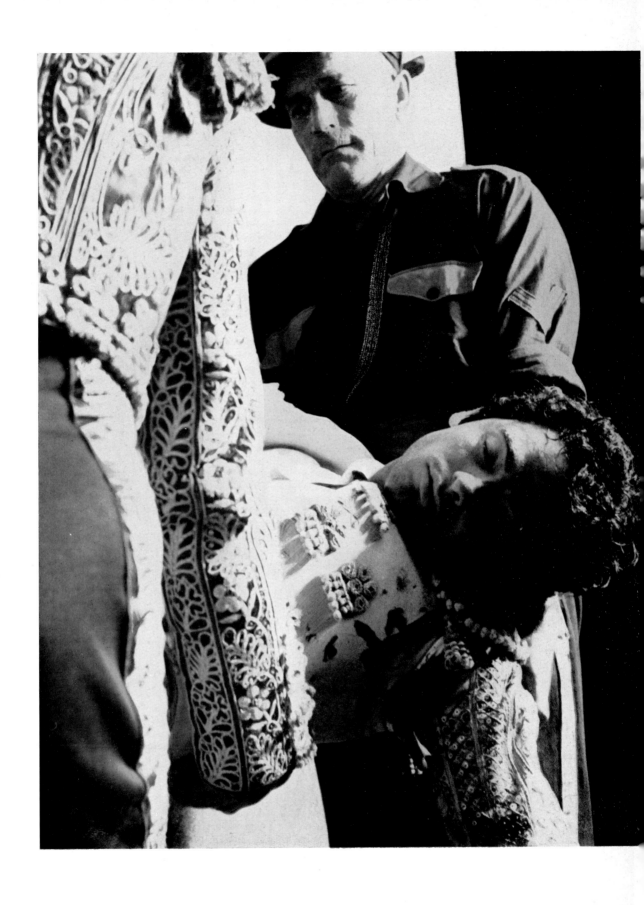

In Moment of Truth Francesco Rosi has created in a lively reconstruction of the life of a toreador a serious and solid work whose polemic is all the stronger for beng understated. The qualities of the form contribute notably to the substance of the narration which, however, is weakened at times by certain brutalities not strictly necessary to the drama.

Francesco Rosi

IL MOMENTO DELLA VERITÀ
MOMENT OF TRUTH

Miguel Mateo Miguelin, Josè Gomez Sevillano, Pedro Besauri Pedrucho, Linda Christian.

ROBERTO ROSSELLINI

Born in Rome on May 8, 1906.

Principal films:

La nave bianca; Un pilota ritorna; L'uomo della Croce; Roma città aperta; Paisà; Amore (La voce umana - Il miracolo); Germania anno zero; La macchina ammazzacattivi; Terra di Dio; Francesco, giullare di Dio; Europa '51; Dov'è la libertà; Viaggio in Italia; Siamo donne; Il Generale Della Rovere; Viva l'Italia; Vanina Vanini; Era notte a Roma.

After being responsible for some of the finest works of the Italian neorealist cinema, in 1959 Roberto Rossellini returned to the theme of the resistance with *General Della Rovere*, a film in which, taking a real event for his subject, he traces a sure psychological picture of an ambiguous character enobled by the drama of the struggle against the Nazis. Rossellini carries this drama forward with the vehemence, the fire, and the resolution of his best moments, without, however, scorning (a new note, indeed) a most happy sense of humor which, at least at the beginning, sketches with subtlest irony the often repellent, but always a little overdrawn figure of the adventurer.

Everything in the story is unfolded with rigorous logic, fertile invention, a wealth of minor characters, very clear dialogue, and an unusually exemplary technique. Above all, Rossellini has taken care that the action never flags, but is sustained at every moment by a sure sense of spectacle, thanks to a skillful use of effects often including suspense. But they are not just catchpenny concessions, for each one always has its own poetic justification.

Indeed, what art there is, what a high sense of drama in the best sequences of this film! Besides the war atmosphere dominating everything with lucid accuracy, besides those bare yet precious pictures renewing the best formal lesson of neorealism, can one possibly recall unmoved the inward subtlety with which the director draws the protagonist's psychological travail, and the balanced, forthright, rugged way he expresses it?

And how can one fail to remember, among the many fine moments in the film, the two grand final scenes? — that last night of the hostages standing up in the common cell, the Jews' prayers, the Pater Noster of the others, and the concluding firing-squad scene to the rhythm of the chaplain's recitation of the *De profundis* which, at first whispered and almost inaudible (over the fallen bodies, the verse *Exaltabunt ossa humiliata*), fills the whole sound-track after the last volley has died away in the air.

A year later (1960), still faithful to the theme of the resistance, in *Era notte a Roma* (*It Was Night in Rome*), Rossellini gives us the story of three allied soldiers hidden in the Rome of the German occupation and generously helped by citizens of every class. Making use of his best neorealist experience of Rome, open city, of the three soldiers, and of all the good people who help them, he gives the clearest and most dramatic of pictures, lurid and often terrible, without abandoning for a moment his proverbial sobriety, directed here, more than formerly, at the same immediacy as the language of television.

Perhaps he can be criticized for some pleonastic moments and, here and there, through his desire to avoid rhetoric altogether, for an excessive haste in "withdrawing" solutions which could have imprinted their emotional or tragic effect a little deeper. Yet it is impossible to deny him once again, not only the ability to be always on the spot with the problems of the day, even with yesterday's stories, but also the happiest gift of being able to achieve poetry even out of nothing. (As for example, during the Christmas dinner in the working woman's home where the three allied soldiers have found refuge, which, at the Russian's sudden emotional outburst at the thought of his country, becomes subtly lyrical.)

Roberto Rossellini

IL GENERALE DELLA ROVERE
GENERAL DELLA ROVERE

Vittorio De Sica, Sandra Milo, Vittorio
Caprioli, Hannes Messemer (Zebra Film,
1959).

Roberto Rossellini

Il generale della rovere
General della rovere

Vittorio De Sica, Sandra Milo, Vittorio
Caprioli, Hannes Messemer (Zebra Film,
1959).

The images of Open City live again in General Della Rovere in the
light of a more refined and mature experience of photography, evoking
a drama which, freed from the immediacy of a news report, takes on
the studied form of the novel.

Roberto Rossellini

Viva l'italia

Renzo Ricci, Paolo Stoppa, Franco In-
terlenghi, Giovanna Ralli, Tina Louise
(Cineriz - Tempo Film - Galatea -
Francinex, 1960).

It Was Night in Rome renews, in similar vein, the experiment of General Della Rovere, while Viva l'Italia tries, at times with success, to apply to traditional history the rough ideas of neorealism and its humble, everyday themes — applying them also to the needs of color photography.

Roberto Rossellini

ERA NOTTE A ROMA
IT WAS A NIGHT IN ROME

Giovanna Ralli, Renato Salvatori, Leo Genn, Paolo Stoppa, Enrico Maria Salerno (International Goldenstar - Film Dismage, 1960).

FRANCO ROSSI

Born in Florence on April 28, 1919.

Principal films:

Il seduttore; Amici per la pelle; Morte di un amico; Odissea nuda; Smog.

After the pleasing success of *Il seduttore* (1954), Franco Rossi won the applause of critics and public at the 1955 Venice Festival with a very charming film, *Amici per la pelle* (*Friends for Life*). A study of the subject of very youthful friendships, made up of give-and-take, sincere affection, but also very sincere outbursts of anger, it touched serene, gentle notes with a human warmth and, at the same time, a simple sincerity rather unusual in Italian cinema.

He was to confront the same theme, but from the point of view of more mature young men, in 1959, with *Morte di un amico* (*Death of a Friend*). This was in part derived from the crude realism of certain films on Roman suburbs and prostitution, but redeemed by an inner morality and a clear, conscious desire to spotlight the burning problems of our contemporary society, not disdaining to indicate concrete solutions without fear of being accused of rhetoric. The style, going beyond the perhaps somewhat external charm of *Friends for Life*, became harder and harsher in contact with a subject examined with an objective, though mostly merciful eye.

But the two films in which Rossi was to make his polemical aims regarding contemporary crises most evident, are the recent *Odissea nuda* (*Naked Odyssey*) (1963) and *Smog* (1962).

Naked Odyssey is a paraphrase of the voyage of Ulysses. Franco Rossi's Ulysses is, in fact, an intellectual who has gone to Tahiti with the definite assignment of making a film (just as Ulysses went to the walls of Troy with the definite task of making war). But as soon as he gets immersed in that climate where the only law (in spite of the European religions and the French language) is the absence of any law, where instincts have free rein and duty is forgotten (because no one imposes it and no one feels it), and life is lived only by instinct, never by conviction, necessity, or obligation towards others, he suddenly gives himself up to the pleasure of simply following nature, at once laying aside every engagement, every responsibility for work. Thus, in less than no time he leaves everything and everybody, and, like the other, the Son of the Myth, he launches out into the "wide open sea," that is, he goes to an even more primitive and lonely island, where there is neither the memory nor the suspicion of civilization.

But while he abandons himself thus to that almost passive state of nature, from far-off Europe there comes news to reawaken his conscience: he thought he had no ties there any more (his marriage had failed years before), but he still had a mother waiting for him, and this mother now dies, lonely and neglected.

Then there, on that island, another affection engages him, paternal this time, for a little boy in need of protection, but if the affection is returned, it is the custom of those places not to accept anything lasting or solid, as it is with us. So one fine day the boy goes off, as calmly and happily as he had come, and the man is left alone: with that bereavement in Europe, that void in his heart, with the discovery that even there, in that carefree paradise, there are people (the missionaries, for example) who believe in duty rather than in pleasure.

And then he returns home. "To pursue virtue and knowledge" one must not run away, escape, or leave the world; rather, one must stick to one's work, to the hard daily round, tied to one's moral and intellectual duties.

It is an odyssey, then, of a wide human and poetic sweep. Perhaps Rossi lingers too much at the beginning over a simple description of the naturalistic life in Tahiti, compiling with too evident pleasure (and without much order) the sequences which will justify his Ulysses "flight." But afterward, when he has followed him through all the psychological stages which will induce him to return, he succeeds in creating moments of genuine emotion. Those, for example, on the mother's death (that Proustian going back over some small detail; that sudden emptiness weighing him down on the island, on the sea, among the palm trees; that lonely wandering on the beach when he feels he has nothing left to hold on to); or those about the little boy, his arrival, his illness which seems so serious, the unspoken joy shining in his eyes, his tricks, his perpetual merriment; or those on the missionaries, deep in quiet recollection, suspended between heaven and earth — scenes inspired (but always without pedantry) by serious considerations of humanity, morality, and religion.

And they are all supported by a photography which — thanks to the stupendous colors and the great depth of the panoramic pictures — really succeed in conveying the more than external charm of the tropics, their secret fascination, often suggested by a particularly appropriate musical accompaniment. And the whole leads to results which, in spite of some unevenness and some gaps, in the end inspire a sincere emotion.

Smog, however, is a solid, serious variation on one of the problems of today most felt by our intellectuals, that is, incommunicability between persons.

The incommunicability with which Rossi deals is not that of Pirandello's plays (which sprang from the impossibility, according to the philosophy of idealism, of knowing the individual truths about anyone), nor is it that wholly existentialist incommunicability which Antonioni's films are about (they take note of his incommunicability without seeking its causes, because the causes would be inherent in the very nature of the man of today). Rather, it is a practical incommunicability the causes of which are carefully investigated and then pointed to in a polemical way, in the attempt to accent those vices and errors which make common life so difficult.

In order to polemicize against these vices and use them as steppingstones to the general problem of today's lack of comprehension among men, Rossi has imagined the story (without a "story") of an Italian traveler who, in changing planes, stops for a few hours in the United States, coming into hasty contact with some of his compatriots: he understands little or nothing of them and does not succeed in entering into real communication with them (as, moreover, neither do they among themselves).

But why is it impossible to have deep, sincere relationships? Certainly not because of the brevity of the meetings. The traveler (a typical member of the conventional, careerist middle classes whose sole aim is to better their social position — entirely taken up with this desire and befogged by a load of provincial commonplaces and clichés about life, society, and his fellows) is not the best person to understand those who, like himself, are just as anxious to succeed in life, but in a different world, in contact with that everyday American reality in which conventionalism, at least, seems outlawed, and the commonplaces on life sound quite the opposite of Italian ones.

But who does our traveler meet? A fine Italian girl who had emigrated to the United States a few years before and has reached a certain economic and social position. In theory, this girl lacks nothing, but it is clear that, to her decidedly sensitive nature, material well-beings is not enough to make people happy. And so we see her become sentimentally interested in a fellow-countryman, but he, consumed with the sole anxiety of getting on, does not really understand what she is aiming at and inevitably disappoints her.

In the end, all three part with a great emptiness in their hearts: the traveler because he, at least, realizes he has disappointed the others, the young man because he sees himself suddenly abandoned by the girl, and the girl because she has seen it is useless to ask others for real help. It is an appeal which will remain unanswered as long as our hearts are filled with the smog of egoism, the blind race after money, the immediate satisfaction of earthly needs.

Thus it has a definite moral and a precise conclusion which dots the *i*'s of every polemical argument. But all this, be it noted, does not give the film a pedantic tone. In fact, Franco Rossi has constructed his story without a story very freely, concentrating particularly on the characters of the three protagonists, the difficulties of their meetings, the misunderstandings often arising from their mutual incomprehension. He has seen to it that these characters (sensitively developed and explained) become the real dynamic force of the action, always using a slow, simple language chiefly aimed at making the states of mind transparent on the screen, but, and this is the important thing, without ever yielding to the poetics of static states of mind produced in merely literary, rarefied atmospheres.

Around these characters from real life he has built up a setting, a framework, a nation — America, which, just because it is always seen with the traveler's eye, and perhaps also under the influence of his often fanciful commonplaces, even in its evident realism comes to have the same dramatic function as the imaginary setting of Kafka's *Amerika*.

Franco Rossi

AMICI PER LA PELLE - FRIENDS FOR LIFE

Geronimo Meynier, Andrea Scirè, Luigi Tosi, Paolo Ferrara, Dina Perbellini (Cines, 1955).

MORTE DI UN AMICO - DEATH OF A FRIEND

Gianni Garko, Spyro Focas, Anna Mazzucchelli. Ilde Mazzucco, Livio Seri, Simonetta Santaniello (Universalcine, '59).

A youthful romantic vein in the service of a tender conflict between two adolescents is seen in Friends for Life; a warmly impassioned, but decidedly realistic style in Death of a Friend, which is a conscious tribute to the needs of a certain realistic type of Italian literature.

Franco Rossi

ODISSEA NUDA - NAKED ODYSSEY

Enrico Maria Salerno, Patricia Dolores Donlon, Venantino Venantini, Nathalie Gasse, Vaca Bennet, Pauline Rey, Elisabeth Logue (P.C.M. Cineriz - Francinex, 1961).

Naked Odyssey: the themes of human search and responsibility — a travel reportage which is really the account of a journey round a tortured conscience, troubled by the problems which disturb the minds of modern intellectuals.

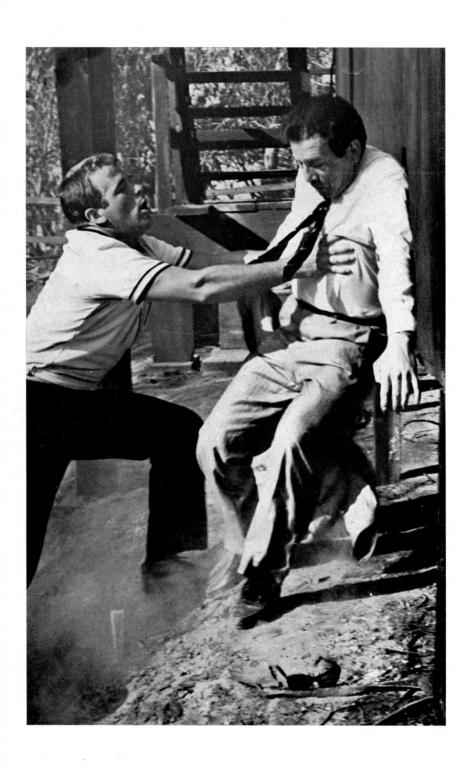

Franco Rossi

Sмog

Enrico Maria Salerno, Annie Girardot,
Renato Salvatori (Titanus - Metro, '62).

Even more definite problems in Smog, where the theme of incommunicability is treated with passionate rigor. In the heart of an almost Kafkian America, three characters who are never able to understand each other, and only hurt each other, are brought together. Developed through a language allusive rather than direct, realistic but intimately symbolic.

180

LUCHINO VISCONTI

Born in Milan on November 2, 1906.

Principal films:

Ossessione; La terra trema; Bellissima; Siamo donne; Senso; Le notti bianche; Rocco e i suoi fratelli; Boccaccio '70 (an episode); Il gattopardo; Vaghe stelle dell'Orsa.

Even when he seems attracted by news reports, Luchino Visconti sticks to literature, his constant preoccupation being to describe reality from a cultural point of view, the only point of view he is interested in as a serious intellectual of refined tastes, informed about everything and interested in everything.

In the immediate postwar period, *The Earth Trembles* had represented the meeting of his cultural tendencies (Flemish in painting, Vergan in literature) with the observation of real life, and, with neorealism in full swing, had signified, if not a turning backward, at least a holding aloof, as a testimony to a deliberately isolated tradition which took lessons from nobody.

On that line, some years afterwards (1954) Visconti confronted history directly in *Senso*, giving us the first real novel in our cinema. Here and there it is questionable because of the presentation of its characters (vaguely drawn from a story by Boito), but it is particularly significant on account of the reversal of the narrative values to which he successfully subjected the structure of the cinema story.

If in 1957 the continuation of this experiment in *Sleepless Nights* (taken from Dostoievski) was to be less significant, he was, however, to achieve happier results in 1960 with *Rocco and His Brothers*. This too, tacitly based on Dostoievski, was a film whose avowed derivation from the forms of the novel — lucidly inserted into the expressive modes of the cinema — carried the already partly successful attempt of *Senso* to a severe completion.

The protagonists in the film are five Lucanian brothers who, after their father dies, let their mother take them off to Milan in the hope they can make a better living there. Four of them are good boys, devoted to their family, their work, and home life in accordance with the customs and patriarchal habits of the South. But one, Simone, is the black sheep and, as luck would have it, the first haunts he chances to frequent are the suburban boxing rings where he at once wins a fair measure of success, and this begins to make him a little swell-headed.

Things are complicated by a meeting with a girl of easy virtue called Nadia, with whom Simone falls in love without, of course, having his tender sentiments returned. Indeed, after a while Nadia tires of Simone's tyrannical ways and leaves him, but by chance, some time after, she runs into Rocco, one of Simone's brothers; she falls in love with him, and this contact with a personality so different from her own decides her to change her way of life. But when Simone realizes this, he lies in wait for the two and attacks Rocco with his fists.

Rocco's reaction is not what one might expect: seeing Simone behave like this, he understands how much Nadia meant to his brother, and he understands, too, why Simone, from the day the girl had gone out of his life, had never been the same and had gone all to pieces in his boxing with one miserable defeat after another. So, with great altruism, he asks Nadia to give up their love and go back to his brother. The girl yields only because Rocco leaves her no choice, but resolves to make Simone's life impossible for him. And that is exactly what happens: heavily in debt, with no more hope in the boxing line, Simone sees himself driven by the woman down the worst slope. So, to find money, there are no depths to which he will not stoop, and he even goes to the length of stealing. He will be saved from prison by his brothers' sticking together, but his fate is sealed: he again runs into Nadia, who has returned to her old way of life, and, blind with rage, he kills her. This time no family solidarity will prevail to arrest the course of justice.

Visconti has divided this material between five great chapters, each one devoted to one of the brothers and arranged in such a way that they do not appear like separate episodes, but rather the homogeneous product of a group story in which, from time to time, certain characters come into the foreground, without the others, though they end up in the background, losing their psychological intensity or their place in the drama. This time his directing, though clearly paying great attention to the photography, has taken particular trouble over the humanity of the characters and this he has always tried to bring out with the greatest care: successful above all in the drawing of Rocco's character, so strangely generous and naïve, sensitive and shy, even in the harshness of certain rebellions, and in the drawing, harder and more incisive, of Simone's character.

The clash between these two characters is responsible for the most intense and violent sequences in the film: Simone's exasperated night attack on Rocco, the harrowing concluding scene where the two brothers, in love with the same woman, are confronted with the horrifying news that one of them has killed her. Less convincing, perhaps, are certain family quarrels, particularly those presided over by the mother (where the stops are pulled out too much, in an atmosphere that is noisy and excited rather than inwardly tragic), and certain merely dialectial attitudes which, in a work of such profound human implications, make one rather suspect an unnecessary polemical pattern.

However, this unevenness is redeemed by the hard realist style (though the realism is of a refined and cultured type) which the director shows above all when he describes a certain foggy Milan, certain streets on the outskirts, certain close-ups of family life (some indoor shots in the Rocco house seem to take us back to the photography of *The Earth Trembles*), and certain group sequences which are often tense to the breaking point.

In 1963 *The Leopard*, from the novel of the same name by Giuseppe di Lampedusa, is a more open continuation of the style of *Senso*, though perhaps *Rocco* remains its more successful conclusion. At the center of the film there is a character who, as in the novel, towers above the others; this is Prince Fabrizio di Salina of Palermo, torn by a personal crisis which is also the crisis of his time.

He is a nobleman of an ancient line who finds himself, by the accident of birth, astride two generations: one which has loyally served the last Bourbons of Naples and Sicily and one which, with the landing of "The Thousand" and the proclamation of the Kingdom of Italy, looks out on a new age, ready to forget the past and make the most of the future. He, however, even though he does not respect the reigning Bourbons, cannot altogether forget the link which bound him to their predecessors, and, as regards the future, he sees the new kingdom too easily made the tool of a caste till yesterday kept at arm's length. So, after a first, contradictory, and almost cynical attempt to come to terms with the new age, he quietly withdraws from it.

In Giuseppe di Lampedusa's text this crisis was followed up to the character's death. The film, however, takes it up to the grand ball offered by the nobility of Palermo in honor of the officers of the Piedmontese army after Aspromonte. It is almost as if it wished that celebration, in which the opposites come together and make peace, to symbolize the end without regrets of one era and the birth of another, perhaps not very different from its predecessor, so showing that for the young and the careerists certain compromises are easy, but for middle-aged persons of serious, not shallow views like the Prince of Salina, they are impossible and only cause bitterness and grief.

This bitterness, this grief pervade the film throughout, from the beginning when the protagonist, though not wishing to interrupt his feudal life (in spite of the Garibaldini first and then the plebiscite), has to submit to meetings and relationships with people who, until a few days before, were his subordinates, and whom now the fashion of the moment actually admits into his family. And later on when, after the first moment of submission to the Piedmontese is over, he realizes how difficult and useless it is to adapt himself to the new regime, and so holds aloof, refusing posts and honors.

In his version, which is quite faithful to the broad lines of the novel, Luchino Visconti has made this bitterness the keynote, drawing it from a succession of situations aimed at suggesting that sense of decay, devastation, and death which was typical of Lampedusa's text. The long, tiring journey, for example, in the blinding summer dust to the villa of Donnofugata, ending with that almost tragic *Te Deum*: a scene which, presenting all the Salinas in the choir stalls, one by one, broken with fatigue, covered with dust, motionless, almost corpselike, gives lurid expression to the atmosphere of decline the whole era is approaching. And, at the end, that sumptuous ball which, with the indirect comment of the protagonist standing aloof, the more gorgeous and uproarious it becomes, the more it seems like a funeral ceremony.

In spite of its apparent gaiety, this is perhaps the sequence which most wrings the heart, recalling most closely that desolate feeling of nostalgia the novel's tensest pages had inspired.

Certainly there are some reservations to be expressed, especially for those pages which, translated onto the screen, have not succeeded in expressing all the author's literary intentions. (The part where Angelica and Tancredi raid the attics at Donnafugata, in the book charged with suspense and feverish sensuality, and by an almost morbid erotic tension heightened by old licentious memories of the place, in the film suffers from the strangeness of the setting, its cobwebs and dusty, rickety furniture making it the real, perhaps the only protagonist in the scene; or again the interview between the Prince and Don Ciccio after the plebiscite, largely emptied of that honest indignation which, in the text, stirred the common people to the depths when they learned their lord was not going to come to terms very nobly with the new regime.) But the film succeeds all the same by virtue of its solemn dramatic atmosphere, giving proof once again of that rich, intelligent style which has put Visconti in the front rank of Italian cinema.

Luchino Visconti

SENSO

Alida Valli, Farley Granger, Massimo
Girotti, Heinz Moog, Rina Morelli
(Lux, 1954).

Senso is the first real "novel" of the Italian cinema, the mature
encounter of Visconti with literature. The occasion for some outstandingly fine photographic experiments.

Luchino Visconti

LE NOTTI BIANCHE - SLEEPLESS NIGHTS

Maria Shell, Marcello Mastroianni, Jean
Marais, Clara Calamai (CI. AS., 1957).

Less effective is the interpretation of Dostoevski given in Sleepless
Nights. But the experiment is particularly valuable as regards the
reconstruction in the studio of settings and scene paintings, in the
manner of Stanislavski's theatre.

186

Luchino Visconti
ROCCO E I SUOI FRATELLI
ROCCO AND HIS BROTHERS

Alain Delon, Renato Salvatori, Annie Girardot, Katina Paxinou, Paolo Stoppa, Roger Hanin, Claudia Mori, Susy Delair, Alessandra Panaro, Corrado Pani, Spyro Focas (Titanus - Les Films Marceau, 1960).

The cinema yicelds to the rhythm of the novel in Rocco and His Brothers a literary text which is unfolded on the screen with a literary rhythm but with a strictly cinematographic language. The photographic experiments of The Earth Trembles are renewed but this time made sounder and more concrete by a greater sense of realism in the composition of the images.

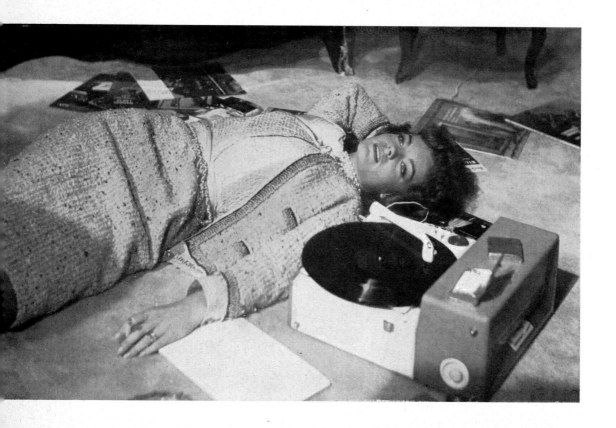

Luchino Visconti

BOCCACCIO '70 (Il lavoro)

Romy Schneider, Tomas Milian, Romolo Valli (Concordia Cinemat. - Cineriz - Francinex Gray Film, 1961).

Maupassant inspires the episode which Visconti has put into Boccaccio '70, a conflict between husband and wife resolved with the graceful wit of the French comic theatre. Withim the limits, of course, of the " divertissement " considerd as an end in itself.

Luchino Visconti

Il gattopardo - The leopard

Burt Lancaster, Claudia Cardinale, A-
lain Delon, Rina Morelli, Paolo Stoppa,
Romolo Valli, Lucilla Morlacchi, Ida
Galli, Serge Reggiani (Titanus, 1963).

Luchino Visconti

IL GATTOPARDO - THE LEOPARD

Burt Lancaster, Claudia Cardinale, A-
lain Delon, Rina Morelli, Paolo Stoppa,
Romolo Valli, Lucilla Morlacchi, Ida
Valli, Serge Reggiani (Titanus, 1963).

**The Leopard is a fresco of Bourbon Sicily at the time of the landing
of "the Thousand." But it is also the completely frank full-length
portrait of the colorful, picturesque figure of the protagonist. Both
aspects of the film are worked out with inspired sympathy and a
richness of photography that is really superb.**

Luchino Visconti

IL GATTOPARDO - THE LEOPARD

Burt Lancaster, Claudia Cardinale, A-
lain Delon, Rina Morelli, Paolo Stoppa,
Romolo Valli, Lucilla Morlacchi, Ida
Galli, Serge Reggiani (Titanus, 1963).

The reconstruction of the period is never external or merely formal;
it deepens themes and meanings, searches out and gives intense expression to social atmospheres and states of mind. It reaches poetic
heights above all in the precise drawing of that sense of decline and
decay emanating from a whole social class, outdated and left high
and dry by the onward flow of history — an onward flow, moreover,
which does not even seem particularly desirable and which, therefore, helps to make the atmosphere poetically pervading, the whole
action even more distressing and sad.

194

Sandra undoubtedly has qualities which make the movie worthy of consideration even though it doesn't reach the dramatic pitch necessary to make the tale acceptable. This tale, although theoretically inspired by a tragedy of Sophocles, is no more than an incestuous story with characters who are somewhat artificial and who are stifled by the complacency of careful direction.

Luchino Visconti

VAGHE STELLE DELL'ORSA - SANDRA

Claudia Cardinale, Jean Sorel, Michael Craig, Marie Bell, Renzo Ricci, Fred William, Amalia Troiani.

LUIGI ZAMPA

Born in Rome on January 2, 1905.

Principal films:

Processo alla città; Anni facili; La Romana; Ladro lui, ladra lei; Il vigile; Anni ruggenti; Frenesie d'Estate; I complessi (an episode).

Luigi Zampa has for some time chosen to be polemical in a humorous vein, although one of the films, after *Anni facili (Easy Years)*, which most attracted the critics' attention was *Woman of Rome*, ambitiously drawn from Moravia's novel of the same name. In general, his attacks are caustic, pointed, and pitiless, but because of the irony they are clothed in, they reach their mark without wounding too much. And this is true whether, taking his cue from a story in the news, he attempts, as in *Il vigile (The Policeman)*, a satire broadly suggested by contemporary morals, or, as in *Anni ruggenti* (The Roaring Years), a parody on a well-known literary text, he caricatures, with firmness but also with taste, the years of the Fascist dictatorship, seen in a mood which, though raising a laugh, is yet not able to free itself deliberately from a disconsolate note of bitterness. And it is all done with rigor, economy, and sincerity.

Nor, on a more directly farcical note, can we forget *Ladro lui, ladra lei*, in which, in 1958, Zampa narrated the exploits, almost in the style of an ironical ballad, of a family of thieves: with a frankly uninhibited verve and lighthearted roguishness which are most enter-taining. The mood, halfway between humor and the grotesque, though very easy, simple, and unsophisticated, is never stale or conventional, so fresh and lively are these caricatures of thieves, so neat, exhilarating, and droll are the various coups pulled off by the jolly protagonist. The son, a simple but also occasionally artful boy, always tries to imitate, step by step, his father's exploits and like him, at every step, always ends up in prison, while the mother, now quite used to the family tradition of coming and going, is calmly indifferent.

Sandwiched between these droll cases, there is also a slight love story — a lady thief who in the end becomes respectable and gets respectably married — but this is the least lively, the weakest, and perhaps the least sincere part of the story. What counts is the rest, the doings of that picturesque tribe of thieves which Zampa unfolds with a very nimble wit and a studied care that never fail. And if, on the one hand, he is never sparing of the most uproarious characters and situations, on the other he has found full scope for pleasing psychological descriptions and delightfully humorous dialogues.

Literature and traditional cinema, the search for a form rather refined in itself, these are Zampa's goals in Woman of Rome.

Luigi Zampa

LA ROMANA - WOMAN OF ROME

Gina Lollobrigida, Daniel Gélin, Franco Fabrizi, Raymond Pellegrin, Xenia Valderi (Ponti De Laurentiis - Excelsa, '54).

Luigi Zampa

IL VIGILE - THE POLICEMAN

Alberto Sordi, Marisa Merlini, Mara
Berni, Nando Bruno, Riccardo Garrone,
Lia Zoppelli (Royal Film, 1960).

Parody and caricature, farce and comedy — Zampa's aspirations in The Policeman and The Roaring Years, two films which, going beyond the restricted limits of farce, achieve wider satirical significance within a decidedly polemical atmosphere.

Luigi Zampa

ANNI RUGGENTI - THE ROARING YEARS

Nino Manfredi, Michele Mercier, Gino Cervi, Salvo Randone, Gastone Moschin, Linda Sini (SPA Cinematografica - Incei Film, 1962).

VALERIO ZURLINI

Born in Bologna on March 19, 1926.

Principal films:

Le ragazze di San Frediano; Estate violenta; La ragazza con la valigia; Cronaca familiare; Le soldatesse.

Valerio Zurlini made his debut with documentaries and then graduated to feature films with *Le ragazze di San Frediano (The Girls of San Frediano)*, a pleasant Florentine ballad, at times rather uneven, but delightfully pervaded by a sincere "group" mood. Later on, in *Estate violenta (Violent Summer)*, he tried to recapture the mood and anxieties of the 25th of July, 1943, but notwithstanding an undeniable rigor of style, he seemed defeated by the passionate nature of themes which in his hands turned into somewhat facile literature.

With *Girl with a Suitcase*, however, he was unanimously hailed as one of the most serious and well-qualified directors of the young Italian school.

It is a film, if you like, with only two characters, but what care, what delicacy, what charm in describing them! He is a boy of good family who has always lived in the dignified quiet of a provincial town like Parma; she is a Milan chorus girl, loud, crude, a woman of the world, though at heart her instincts of decency are fundamentally sound. He falls in love with her, almost without knowing it, and without realizing she is not exactly a pure maiden; but, of course, things do not go smoothly, and the girl, who happens to be in Parma because of a dirty trick played on her by his brother, goes back to the seaside resort she had left.

Soon after, the young man follows her, though he knows very well this move will get him nowhere, and, realizing that the girl is in financial straits, in order to make up for his brother's bad turn, he secretly leaves her a little money. Then he goes sadly away, so closing with calm dignity the only chapter of his "first love."

The strength of the film, however, does not lie in the story which, told like this, would seem like another edition of the time-worn theme of the boy of good family and the chorus girl. Rather, it is in the sensitive way in which it presents the gradual unfolding of the innocent young man's silent, pure, honorable love, and in the human warmth with which it builds up the character of the experienced but not vicious girl, and her increasingly astonished reactions to his devotion which, at first, she cannot even understand.

Zurlini has poised this encounter with exquisite care, has constructed it with the keenest psychological insight, and has described it with an almost ethereal inwardness, in a mood where sensitive modesty is linked to a sweet, austere reserve. Unfortunately, after the first part, where it is perfectly timed, the story loses a good deal of its charm and goes to pieces somewhat as a narrative (and also as regards the tautness and concentration of the mood), but this does not altogether lessen its value, because of its presentation of the unusual Parma setting and the dry intensity of the dialogue with never a single flaw.

But Zurlini's most serious and accomplished work is *Cronaca familiare (Family History, 1962)*, drawn from Vasco Pratolini's novel of the same name.

The story, as Pratolini's readers know, simply consists in the narration of a family history by an elder brother, speaking directly to a younger brother who has died but is still alive in his memory. In the novel this narration, not in the third or first, as usually happens, but in the second person ("When Mother died you were only twenty-five days old, and were already far away

200

from her on the hill") was not a mere pretext for trying to be original, but a lively way of ensuring the direct, continual presence in the story not only of the real protagonist, i.e., the dead brother, but also and above all of the bond between the two brothers, in the light of which Pratolini was writing.

In the film, which as regards the story is an intelligent and faithful copy of the novel (even in the dialogue), this narration in the second person is made by the voice of the speaker, and so the atmosphere of the family bond, which the author intended to create with this device, remains perfectly expressed. This bond lights up the whole story, keeping it always in a moving atmosphere and kindling in it moments of the deepest pathos. But how?

The "things" to be told were not many: a baby is born, the mother dies; the brother, the father, and the grandmother put him out to nurse in the house of a rich gentleman where he is brought up like a son. The years pass, the father dies, the elder brother, who is poor, puts the grandmother in an old people's home and leaves Florence (where most of the action takes place), at the same time leaving the younger brother in the house of his foster father. Some time afterwards he comes back, still poor, and ill. The two brothers meet and the younger, who has an angelic nature (the other is more complicated, harder, perhaps a little selfish) arranges for the family to unite, at least from time to time, around the grandmother. Then the grandmother dies too, the younger brother marries, but it is an unhappy marriage, he falls ill, the war comes, the illness is mysterious and hard to cure, the elder brother does everything to save him, but in vain. And his brother dies.

These flat, simple things, which Pratolini had already narrated with crystal clarity in what are perhaps the neatest and best pages he has written as a successful writer, Zurlini has recreated on the screen. He has endeavored to make them vibrate with the same intense, concentrated emotion as Pratolini had given them, basing the photography (it is a color film) on the paintings of Rosai in order to represent the geometrical harmonies and well-ordered architecture of the Florentine backgrounds; and seeking a wisely slow and amply cadenced rhythm, using pauses and deliberately suspending the movement in calm periods of recollection in order to produce the moods desired, the most harrowing but also the most secret, intimate, unexpressed moments in the story.

The sequence, for example, of the first meeting between the two brothers and the grandmother at the old people's home: exemplary from every point of view, in the center of a set reduced to bare essentials, it isolates the trio who, almost without speaking, with very slow gestures and long sustained pauses, finally meet and mingle in a unique feeling of tenderness and joy. Here, as in other moments in the film, Zurlini could have yielded to rhetoric, to an exaggerated accentuation of "good things," and to sentimentality. Instead, he always maintains a firmly controlled taste and, when he quietly reaches the right moment, he suddenly stops and tells the story chiefly from within, externalizing it as little as possible, aiming always and with rigor at a poetry of unsaid things or of things barely intimated. And with a lyricism which does not reject realism, a sensitivity which never fails to be rigorous, and a warmth which is always accompanied by severity.

Valerio Zurlini

ESTATE VIOLENTA - VIOLENT SUMMER

Eleonora Rossi Drago, Jean Louis Trintignant, Lilla Brignone, Raf Mattioli,
Nadia Gray, Jaqueline Sassard (Titanus, 1959).

The crisis of July 1943, political, historical, human: Violent Summer.
Uneven in the narrative, yet it reveals in Zurlini a dramatic zeal which
points clearly to his future possibilities.

Valerio Zurlini

LA RAGAZZA CON LA VALIGIA
GIRL WITH A SUITCASE

Claudia Cardinale, Jacques Perrin, Luciana Angiolillo, Corrado Pani, Riccardo Garrone, Renato Baldini, Romolo Valli (Titanus - S.G.C., 1960).

A conflict between an adolescent and a fille de joie expressed with great delicacy and very sensitive psychological insight: Girl with a Suitcase. In a provincial setting which Zurlini evokes with a master hand, more alive to the inner mental attitudes of the world it depicts than their surface appearances.

Valerio Zurlini

CRONACA FAMILIARE - FAMILY HISTORY

Marcello Mastroianni, Jacques Perrin, Salvo Randone, Serena Vergano, Valeria Ciangottini (Titanus - Metro, 1962).

Literature and cinema perfectly blended with a congenial sensitivity: Family History. Pratolini's text becomes pure cinema; Zurlini translates it onto the screen with lucid skill. From a visual point of view, he links it to the severest modern Italian painting, while, from a narrative point of view, he maintains it in a literary climate of noble clarity. In the pauses, in the balance of the rhythm, in the sensitive search for the most inward and intimate states of mind, he brings it to the same poetic heights to which the writer had originally brought it, constructing a spectacle of exemplary perfection.

Marco Bellocchio
Bernardo Bertolucci
Tinto Brass
Franco Brusati
Pasquale Festa Campanile
Vittorio Caprioli
Damiano Damiani
Marco Ferreri
Massimo Franciosa
Ugo Gregoretti
Gualtiero Jacopetti
Nanni Loy
Francesco Maselli
Ermanno Olmi
Valentino Orsini
Vito Pandolfi
Pier Paolo Pasolini
Giuseppe Patroni Griffi
Elio Petri
Gillo Pontecorvo
Folco Quilici
Brunello Rondi
Luciano Salce
Paolo e Vittorio Taviani
Florestano Vancini
Eriprando Visconti
Lina Wertmüller

While the leading creators of the Italian cinema were pursuing their own paths, marked sometimes by a certain regression but more often by definite advances in technique and language, the younger creators were making their reputations, each one according to his own personality and in general faithful to his own principles and aesthetic aims amid the surrounding welter of other inclinations, aspirations, and tendencies, often immediately successful even with a first film, made usually at the end of a serious training in the field of the documentary.

For instance: Ermanno Olmi, who must certainly be counted among the foremost in this group and is undoubtedly the most promising. He made his debut with a short film, *Time Has Stopped*, simply by telling the story of two men cut off in the snow in the deep Bergamo valleys with a careful, almost minute observation of reality. He succeeded in creating a genuine poetic atmosphere, embracing a limpid psychological analysis, at once sensitive and severe.

Graduating to feature films with *The Sound of Trumpets*, he displayed a still more mature and warmer human experience and style. The subject of the film was, in appearance, modest. It was based on the long procedure a young man from the suburbs of Milan had to go through before being hired by an industrial firm, and on the long probationary period he had to endure after being hired, before beginning to climb, one by one, the rungs of the clerk's career.

But to develop such a simple theme, Olmi evoked the great world of little things on the screen with delightful sensitivity, revealing himself an observer at once careful and subtle, inspired and sympathetic, able to gather the poetic feeling of the humblest details of daily life and also, in another direction, to discover in the hearts of his characters the echoes, perhaps hidden but nonetheless alive, of the most expansive feelings. And he describes them all with a calm, refined language, always alive to the suggestions of the realist lesson, but always careful not to sacrifice to it a human discovery, a psychological explanation, a state of mind of romantic origin.

In his latest film, *The Fiancés*, these unimpeachable stylistic virtues seem marred by an obscure, sometimes convincing story, but they bear witness all the same to a personality which, in the long run, will not be a disappointment.

After two early films, done in a facile, not very careful style (*L'audace colpo dei soliti ignoti* and *Un giorno da leoni — A Day for Lion-hearts*), Nanni Loy attracted the attention of critics and public alike with an outstandingly dramatic work, *The Four Days of Naples*, an objective, passionately moving account of those four glorious days in September 1943 when the people of Naples, more with the force of desperation than with arms, succeeded, unaided, in forcing the Nazis to leave the city even before the Allies liberated it.

It is a symphonic film where every episode, always based on strictly authentic records, tends to blend with the others so that the variety of its situations, the multiplicity of its characters, and the diversity of its states of mind reach a unity imposed and inspired by that collective impulse which drove the people of Naples, exhausted though they were by privations and the bombardments, to rise up and triumph.

The action is very skillfully timed because, as it follows the events of those days step by step, at first it moves slowly in the elated atmosphere of the armistice, then it begins to quicken its pace in a feverish dramatic crescendo as the Germans occupy the city, shoot hostages, and carry out raids, and finally, as a stream on its way to the sea swells into a great river, the revolt is organized from house to house, breaks out and overflows, until on the fourth day it at last sees the *Wermacht* hoist the white flag.

Loy has expressed this crescendo with an agitated, often overpowering rhythm, perhaps allowing himself too many individual pauses and, here and there, though avoiding rhetoric, not restraining an excessive sentimentality in view of the too freely flowing tears, but achieving all the same solid dramatic results, thanks to a photography which, openly inspired by the plain, unadorned pictures of the war newsreels and documentaries, gives on every page the feeling not just of veracity but of authenticity.

Right from the moment of his first film, *Lipstick*, Damiano Damiani has won critical attention because of his calm, certain language, with which he successfully attempted a detective story without falling into any of the commonplaces of the genre. The psychological descriptions are felicitous, and the characters, including the minor ones, are unusually lifelike.

The same is true, later, of *Il sicario*, where he showed particular maturity in dealing with rather uncertain settings. So, too, but in the more ambitious and risky attempt at a definite literary adaptation, in *Arturo's Island*, which, without giving thorough expression to the poetic undercurrents in Elsa Morante's text, did touch on some intensely lyrical moods with strict equilibrium, and was only occasionally embarrassed by a failure to master the difficult psychological developments in the story.

Less successful, however, was the attempt to manage groups in *The Get-together*, a sort of "night out" of a group of forty-year-olds vainly seeking to recapture the feelings of earlier days in all their authentic freshness. Literary and naive, the film sketches the most ill-assorted characters and situations without any force, leading them to obvious, inevitable conclusions, with a slow, tedious, discursive rhythm (though the unity of time tries conscientiously to give it depth and concentration).

The Empty Canvas is successful only as entertainment for the general public. A not very faithful adaptation of Moravia's novel of the same name, the film destroys almost all its philosophical meanings, transforming it into a shallow love story pervaded by the most conventional pangs of jealousy. Psychological motivations are almost nonexistent.

Another director who has not yet found a style of his own is Elio Petri, who, to date, has three films to his credit: *The Murder, Days Are Numbered,* and *The Schoolteacher from Vigevano.* The first, polemical, strong, and decided, satisfied all the requirements of intelligent spectacle with a language which, although a first attempt, already showed itself quite firm and mature, with a feast, too, of photographic delights.

The second deliberately took its stand against the run on conventional canons of film-making, and dared to base itself entirely on the drama of a man who felt death near and feebly tried to fight it. The language was even more inspired and mature, more alive to expressive technique, more anxious for novelty, more interested in pictorial composition (though within its realistic needs), more free from fixed schemes, trite narrative modes, and old, outworn prescriptions.

The Schoolteacher from Vigevano, the third film, while certainly the most ambitious, shows the ambiguous effects of an excessively literary basis: these are the result partly of Lucio Mastronardi's novel of the same title from which the film is drawn, and partly of the downright symbolist intentions with which Petri has worked it out.

However, it reveals a definite talent for style and a care for psychology which, even when it takes the characters to the verge of the grotesque and, often, of caricature, yet pays attention to their humanity, expressing this in a bitter, subtle mood.

Florestano Vancini is more rigorous, but he too seems to be unsure about which path to follow. Unlike other directors, his work seems handicapped by his documentary experience. In *The Long Night of '43,* in fact, his taste for pictorial composition and his inclination to observe settings and landscapes in the foreground have prevented him from really focusing on the characters, though these qualities have at the same time enabled him to present states of mind blended with surroundings in compositions that are worthy of much praise.

In *The Casaroli Gang* the lack of balance is less noticeable, and the characters, caught up in the giddy whirl of a very topical passage, are more in the foreground, but, to be made complete, they would still need that sense of psychological development which Vancini

clearly neglects in favor of the peripheral elements. Even so, he is already making his mark with a certain force of personality.

The contemporary record of the Italian film — which is not and cannot yet become history — has been marked by a curious and interesting phenomenon which we feel we must point out at the end of these notes on the activity of our principal creators and the younger generation who have followed them. It is the phenomenon of the beginners, of those, that is, who have often succeeded in bringing themselves to the notice of the critics with their first films, particularly through the help of the Venice Film Festival since the *Biennale* added the " First Films " class for those taking part in the competition, precisely to mark the serious and often successful work done by young beginners in the cinema today.

These first films, naturally, are often marred either by the youth, by the technical inexperience, or by that excess of ambition which is often keener in the immature than in the successful, but it would be unfair not to note that, in our opinion, they securely represent the promise of the Italian cinema of tomorrow.

Coming, like so many others, to feature films from documentaries, Francesco Maselli brings to the cinema an intellectual zeal and literary leanings which, though not always finding happy outlets in the stories, each time enable him (in *The Stragglers, The Woman of the Day,* and *The Dolphins*) to create sequences of sustained brilliance as far as the photography is concerned.

Maselli is a director with a firm grip and, even when the text is not convincing, he redeems it with a highly personal study of the characters and a pictorial severity in presenting settings and landscapes worthy of the best school.

In this regard, his presentation of Italian provincial life in *The Dolphins* is definitely characteristic.

It is questionable, however, how faithfully the film follows Moravia's text, *Gli indifferenti (The Time of Indifference),* on which it is based. Maselli's film has telescoped the text, in a style which may be somewhat self-conscious, but in which the barrenness, discomfort, desolation, and cynicism of the characters often come into sharp focus with much the same force as in the original literary text.

Although Gillo Pontocorvo, has but one film to his credit, *Kapò,* he deserves a place among the top-ranking directors from whom the critics have come to expect a great deal.

His film, set in a concentration camp, is centered on the character of a woman who is promoted from prisoner to trustee and, through fear of the sufferings she has undergone, becomes harsher, fiercer, and crueler than the guards — a character who moves and horrifies from beginnning to end with a force, a rigor, and a tragic tension of a very high level.

Perhaps the psychological portrait of the protagonist is clearer and more successful at the beginning, when it follows the woman's first change into a brute, than at the end, when it traces the second, more inevitable change of the brute into a woman. But even so, the film is gripping because of its heart-rending atmosphere of atrocities, because of its sinister characters always constructed with a proportion which even the most realistic horrors cannot overwhelm, and above all, because of its painful inquiry into human nature which, without external polemics, simply states the degradation a human being can reach through terror.

His promising beginning notwithstanding, Ugo Gregoretti is still an unknown quantity. In his first episode film, *The New Angels*, he showed that he had a great deal of shrewdness, creative inspiration, and fantasy in his make-up, and is equally good at making an inquiry into social backgrounds or composing an ironical, satirical sketch.

He graduated to the feature film with *Omicron*. Although he attracted attention for his ingenious idea of basing science fiction on real life, he was not able to free himself from a certain polemical obsession which transformed his pleasing scherzo into a political diatribe.

Pier Paolo Pasolini aims to have a place apart from this group. A contradictory and complicated figure — poet, writer, cinema director — Pasolini has caught the attention of the critics with three films, *The Beggar*, *Mamma Roma*, and *The Gospel According to Matthew*. All three have aroused discussion and are controversial, but, in spite of certain errors of taste and narrative structure, they cannot but reveal the clear intention to blend culture (literature and painting) with cinematic realism, in the manner of the experiment already successfully attempted by Luchino Visconti in *The Earth Trembles*.

This intention has given good results particularly in some sequences in *The Beggars*, sustained by an intense vigor in the photography, and in some passages of *Mamma Roma*, but these latter are marred by an intellectualism which often strips them of a good deal of their authenticity.

In *The Gospel*, on the other hand, a film loosely based on the Biblical text, Pasolini's patent intention was to create a cinematographic effect nearer to the oratorio in feeling than to a dramatic account. His attempts in this direction robbed the characters of their depth and of much of their vitality, with the result that he has created a film whose most imaginatively intense moments serve only to elucidate events, which are always propounded, never narrated.

Pasolini's student and assistant, Bernardo Bertolucci, uses an original subject of Pasolini's for his first film, *The Thin Gossip*, constructed on the investigations carried out by the police after the murder of a prostitute. He creates a particularly tense dramatic atmosphere with flat, simple means almost entirely the result of careful, minute observation which, however, is never remote from reality and makes him very plainly a member of the neorealist school. But, though his creating is influenced by respect for factual records, he gives them a warmer human atmosphere in which even the most unpleasant characters and the crudest situations take on acceptable outlines. His language — though excessively free or overly intellectual or too vague or not always altogether authentic, attentive as it is to pauses, tense moments, flashbacks charged with question marks and suspense — succeeds nevertheless in visualizing the plot with undoubted originality and with a more refined photography than is usual with realist narrators.

Among the young directors, Eriprando Visconti has given us accomplished work, provocative, full of promise, ever since his first film, *A Story in Milan*. This is the portrait of a middle-class girl of the present day who carries her opposition to convention in any form to the point of refusing to marry the man she loves, who has seduced her, simply because she knows he has proposed marriage only in deference to a conformist mentality.

It is a polemical, but not gratuitously rebellious, portrait, drawn in an original way. Focusing on the protagonist's character and presenting her little by little, surprising her in the middle of the rather frivolous world that welcomes her, in the round of society parties, in the bosom of vague, abstracted families, among unfeeling, shallow friends, within little drawing-room intrigues, he breaks the story into many dissimilar episodes, which he then skillfully resolves in a single narrative unity, a compact dramatic atmosphere — and the principal character is finally presented in her every subtle nuance.

Folco Quilici's psychological aims soon made him leave documentary for the feature film, where he has been making reportage films for some time. From *Sixth Continent* to *Last Paradise* and his latest *Ti-Koyo and His Shark*, he has always tried to find in his beloved tropical landscapes human elements from which to produce an inner drama.

The best results he obtained on these lines were with *Ti-Koyo*, in which, blending reality with fable, truth with absurdity, he succeeded in giving us a story which is often enchanting, uniting, as it does, the charm of South Sea landscapes with the tenderness of a psychological encounter resolved with delicate balance. Although the atmosphere is avowedly derived from a literary text, it always maintains the genuine, immediate flavor of life.

Into the documentary and reportage field (successfully initiated by the poetical wanderings of Giangaspare Napolitano, Enrico Gras, Mario Craveri, Bonzi, and Lualdi), Gualtiero Jacopetti has brought a new note, pointed and polemical, shrewd and forceful, evident above all in his *Mondo Cane*, which was soon imitated in his own and other sequels that deliberately juxtapose the most contradictory, harsh, and violent aspects of our times, thus transforming the placidly agreeable travelogue into a work which is often perverse in taste but always exercises a strange and intense fascination.

Among the stage directors who in the fast few years have tried, with varying degrees of success, to make names for themselves in film, Franco Brusati and Giuseppe Patroni Griffi should be mentioned.

Brusati, after a somewhat literary adaptation of Alfredo Panzini's *Il padrone sono me* in *The Boss*, ran the risk of paraphrasing, this time in a Milanese setting, Fellini's *La dolce vita* with his film *Disorder*.

Notwithstanding the unevenness of the narrative, its derivation from another work, and its intellectualist slant, this film has the merit of a rich, cinematographic language full of body, in some places really calligraphic and baroque, but in general solid and effective, which makes the characters and settings stand out clearly, even though the inequalities of the narration often empty them of real humanity.

The latter, Patroni Griffi, in spite of his successes in the theatre, has not made a god start in the cinema. In fact, *The Sea*, his first film, a tortured drama of sentimental misunderstandings set in Capri in winter, fails to make us experience the concrete humanity of the characters who are suffocated under symbolism and literary allusion that communicate nothing and lack authenticity. The failure of the characters to communicate extends even to the viewer and expresses, therefore, nothing but itself, even though, from the technical point of view, the film has some noteworthy stylistic passages.

Among the memorable imitators we must list the brothers Paolo and Vittorio Taviani and Valentino Orsini who first came before the public with a work of collaboration, a film of decided promise, *A Man to Burn*, which is a fictionalized version of a true story about a Sicilian trade unionist whose character is neither altogether good nor altogether bad, neither altogether heroic nor altogether cowardly. Thus his behavior in life and politics is very contradictory and often questionable, occasioning more criticism than approval in friends and enemies alike, until one day an inner impulse of revolt drives him to do things that antagonize the Mafia, and so he is in danger of being eliminated at any moment.

But the interest of the subject is not matched with equal interest in the way it is handled because, although the three directors here and there manage some tersely realistic sequences that are particularly successful in reconstructing the setting, they often display a language clipped to the point of crudity and a stylistic imprecision which puts factual reporting alongside fine imagery, strict documentary next to the rustic sketch.

In the group of comic creators, Luciano Salce and Vittorio Caprioli deserve mention.

Salce comes from the theatre, not so much to drama inclined toward comedy as to caricature of contemporary manners, as he has revealed in *The Federal* and *Crazy Desire*. His one attempt at a more severe analysis of the psychological disturbances of our age, in *Hours of Love*, very felicitously dwells, in a manner only disguisedly ironical, upon that incompatibility between husband and wife which is at present one of the most deeply felt themes in our cinema.

With Caprioli too the lure of farce is often overcome by an interest in the comedy of manners and study of the characters, with results that, even when not entirely convincing, cause a certain attention to be paid to him. For example: *Dear Paris*, which was designed to fit the acting of Franca Valeri, manages to strike some rather nice ironical notes in spite of the flimsiness of the story. And the first episode of *Cuori infranti*, "La mano di Fatma," again made for Franca Valeri, creates a curious figure, developed pleasantly and with verve.

Finally, among contemporary film talents, beginners and those already established, we should not overlook the following (even though their most recent films do not satisfy all our expectations): Massimo Franciosa and Pasquale Festa Campanile, for their literary achievements in which, after years of highly successful screenwriting, they have attempted a very modern conjugal triangle in *Sentimental Experiment;* Tinto Brass, for the fantastic vibrancy with which he has portrayed (in *At the Time of the World*) the melancholy biography of a young man at the crossroads of life, seen in a highly personal way; Marco Ferreri, who won considerable critical approval with *The Conjugal Bed* (also released as *The Queen Bee*), a remarkable parody of a marriage, worked out with debatable accents here and there, along the lines of a macabre comedy which more than once encroaches on the grotesque; Lina Wertmüller, of the rural and provincial "slice of life" of *The Basilisks*, which is flawed with realist bitterness; Brunello Rondi, for the austerity with which (in *Il demonio*) he has balanced the topics and problems of Southern Italy, considered in ethnographic terms, with the anguish of real-life characters, involved in their own highly personal drama; and Vito Pandolfi who, in *The Last*, treats the stories of a poor family of Venetian peasants, and who showed that he still accepted the neorealist lesson concerning the thoroughly documentary style of narration and concerning the immediacy with which reality is sought and expressed, but at the same time displayed a decided tendency to enhance every frame with a studied imaginative dignity.

1963

ITALIE FRANCE

COMÉDIE DRAMATIQUE

LE LIT CONJUGAL
UNA STORIA MODERNA : L'APE REGINA

RÉALISATEUR
Marco Ferreri

LE LIT CONJUGAL

Réalisation	Marco FERRERI (1963)
Scénario	Rafael AZCONA, M. FERRERI
Avec la collaboration de	Diego FABRI, Pasquale FESTA CAMPANILE, Massimo FRANCIOSA
D'après une idée de	Goffredo PARISE
Directeur de la photographie	Ennio GUARNIERI
Musique	Teo USUELLI
Production	Sancro Film - Fair Film (Rome) Films Marceau Cocinor (Paris)
Distribution	Cocinor
Durée	95 minutes

INTERPRÉTATION

Regina	Marina VLADY
Alfonso	Ugo TOGNAZZI
Le père Mariano	Walter GILLER
Mafalda	Achille MAJERONI
La mère supérieure	Linda SINI
Igi	Igi POLIDORO
Riccardo	Riccardo FELLINI
Don Giuseppe	Pietro TATTANELLI
Jolanda	Vera RAGAZZI

L'HISTOIRE

Quand un homme atteint la quarantaine et qu'il a bien vécu, il aspire à se ranger, à se marier. C'est ce qui arrive à Alfonso, soucieux néanmoins de ne pas se tromper : sa femme doit être belle mais aussi religieuse, pleines de principes et, si possible, vierge. C'est le Père Mariano, un vieil ami d'Alfonso, qui va dénicher l'oiseau rare, Regina, tout près du Dôme de Saint-Pierre à Rome, dans une famille bourgeoise autant que dévote. Regina ne se donnera à Alfonso qu'après le mariage et, bien entendu, pour avoir tout de suite un enfant.

Mais cet enfant n'arrive pas. Pourtant, la jeune femme le désire ardemment et met tout en œuvre pour que son époux le lui fasse. Heureux d'abord de trouver une épouse aussi disposée à accomplir le plus souvent possible son devoir conjugal, Alfonso ne tarde pas à éprouver quelques défaillances. Qu'à cela ne tienne, Regina redouble de séduction pour redonner courage et énergie à son homme. Rien n'y fait ; aucun heureux événement en vue.

Alfonso, qui dépérit, doit subir un traitement à base de piqûres d'hormones. En vain. Il ne fait plus maintenant que ce qu'il peut, astreint à une nouvelle forme de travaux forcés, ceux de l'amour. Enfin, Regina est enceinte. Victime d'une crise cardiaque, son devoir accompli, Alfonso est abandonné dans un coin, à demi impotent. Il ne lui reste plus qu'à contempler sa femme, radieuse, qui prépare la venue au monde de son héritier.

LA PETITE HISTOIRE

Ape regina *signifie, en italien,* la reine des abeilles. *Ferreri, d'ailleurs, le rappelle clairement qui termine son film par cette citation de Shakespeare :* « Apporter à la ruche son butin et recevoir la mort pour salaire, tel fut le sort du père expirant. » *Il va de soi que ce film fit scandale (il fut « retenu » plusieurs mois par la censure) dans l'Italie des années soixante où l'institution du mariage était toujours sacro-sainte et où l'idée même du divorce et à plus forte raison celle de la contraception* suscitaient les foudres de la toute puissante hiérarchie de l'Église catholique. Ce premier long métrage de Ferreri en Italie, après trois films réalisés en Espagne d'après des scénarios d'Azcona, EL PISITO (Le petit appartement, 1958), LOS CHICOS (1959) et EL COCHECITO (La petite voiture, 1960), n'en représenta pas moins le cinéma italien au Festival de Cannes 1963 où Marina Vlady se vit décerner le Prix d'interprétation féminine pour son rôle de Regina.

Bernardo Bertolucci

LA COMMARE SECCA - THE THIN GOSSIP

Nonprofessional actors (Compagnia
Cinematografica Cervi, 1962).

Giuseppe Patroni Griffi

IL MARE

Umberto Orsini, Françoise Prévost, Dino
Mele (Gianni Buffardi, 1962).

Hard, bitter sequences, dictated by the style of first-hand reporting
but enriched by photographic aims which come near to art; language
which, in spite of certain rawnesses due to inexperience, makes a serious attempt at style — this is Bertolucci's The Thin Gossip, a variation on Pasolini's themes, but developed with insights that are altogether personal. Symbols, literature, intellectual attitudes, reflected in
images which often show a baroque emphasis — such is Patroni Griffi's
The Sea, a debatable film, but one not without linguistic achievements.

Giovanni Tinto Brass

CHI LAVORA È PERDUTO
WHO WORKS IS LOST
Sady Rebbot, Pascale Audret, Tino
Buazzelli (Zebra Film, 1963).

Intellectualism, autobiography, bohemianism, but also a sense of cinema, pungent irony, and outstanding narrative talent are evident in
Who Works Is Lost, a film which reveals a newcomer, Tinto Brass,
with a sure future.

Franco Brusati

IL DISORDINE - DISORDER
Samy Frey, Louis Jourdan, Antonella
Lualdi, Tomas Milian, Renato Salva-
tori, Jean Sorel, Susan Strasberg, Alida
Valli, Georges Wilson (Titanus - Société
Nouvelle Pathé Cinéma, 1962).

A baroque image, composite and exuberant, a style charged with
symbols and visual meanings, but a not altogether original theme,
often overburdened with excessively literary intentions: Brusati's
Disorder.

Marco Bellocchio

PUGNI IN TASCA

Lou Castel, Paola Pitagora, Marino Masé, Pierluigi Troglio, Liliana Gerace, Jennie Mac Neil (Doria Cinematografica, 1965).

Pugni in Tasca (Fists in the Pocket), the first work of the youthful Marco Bellocchio, is the dramatic account of a personal history of morbid relationships delineating extreme psychological phenomena in a provincial setting. It brings great sensitivity to bear on an abnormal environment that has been rendered acceptable and comprehensible through the simplicity of its portrayal.

Ironical comedy and playful farce in Caprioli's films. Usually made as a vehicle for Franca Valeri, a star who in the Italian cinema has borne the weight of a many-sided personality, full of ironic temperament.

Vittorio Caprioli

PARIGI O CARA... - DEAR PARIS

Franca Valeri, Vittorio Caprioli, Margherita Girelli, Fiorenzo Fiorentini, Anna Maria Ubaldi, Antonio Battistella (Ajace Cinematografica, 1963).

Damiano Damiani

IL ROSSETTO - LIPSTICK

Pierre Brice, Giorgia Moll, Laura Vivaldi, Pietro Germi, Bella Darvi (Europa Cinematografica - Explorer Film
C.F.P.C., 1960).

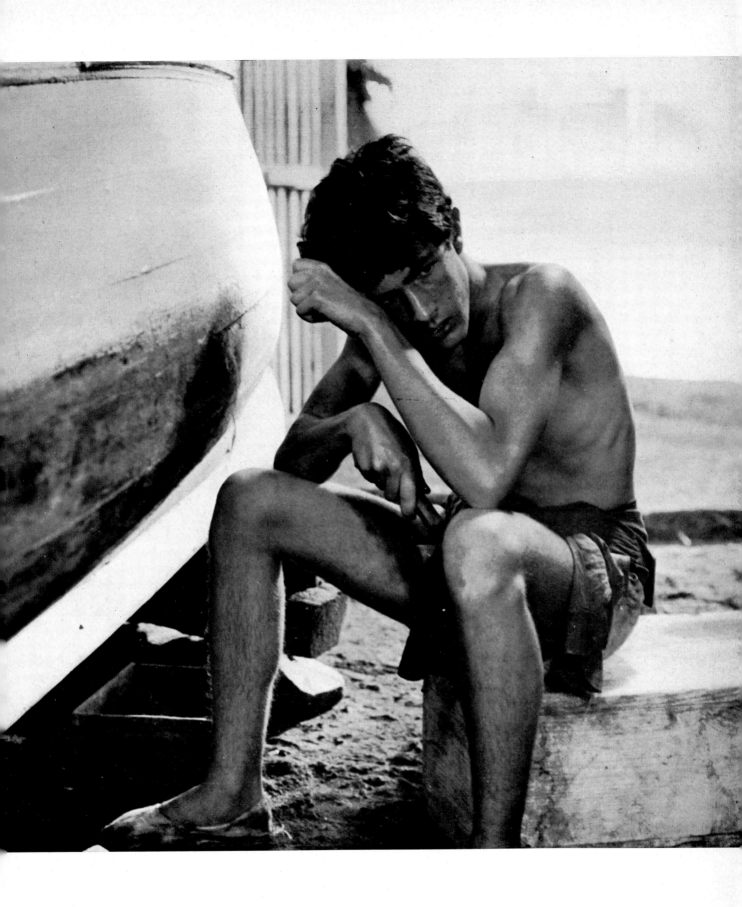

In spite of the severe literary inspiration (Elsa Morante's novel), in Arturo's Island Damiani does not go beyond the exercise of style. At times, however, he displays a happy sensitivity in evoking characters, conflicts, states of mind.

Damiano Damiani

L'isola di arturo - Arturo's island

Reginald Kernan, Vanni de Maigret, Kay Meersman, Luigi Giuliani (Champion S.p.A., 1961).

221

Damiano Damiani

LA RIMPATRIATA - THE GET-TOGETHER

Walter Chiari, Leticia Roman, Francisco Rabal, Riccardo Garrone, Paul Guers, Mino Guerrini, Dominique Boschero (Galatea - 22 Dicembre, 1963).

LA NOIA - THE EMPTY CANVAS

Catherine Spaak, Horst Bucholtz, Bette Davis (Champion Film, 1964).

The Get-Together disintegrates into a set of forced groupings from which merely programmatic characters emerge in an atmosphere of sentimentality which deadens any realist intention. The Empty Canvas, on the contrary, translates Moravia's difficult novel into a merely commercial vein and displays it to the public with a correct sense of spectacle, although forgetting all its inner motivation.

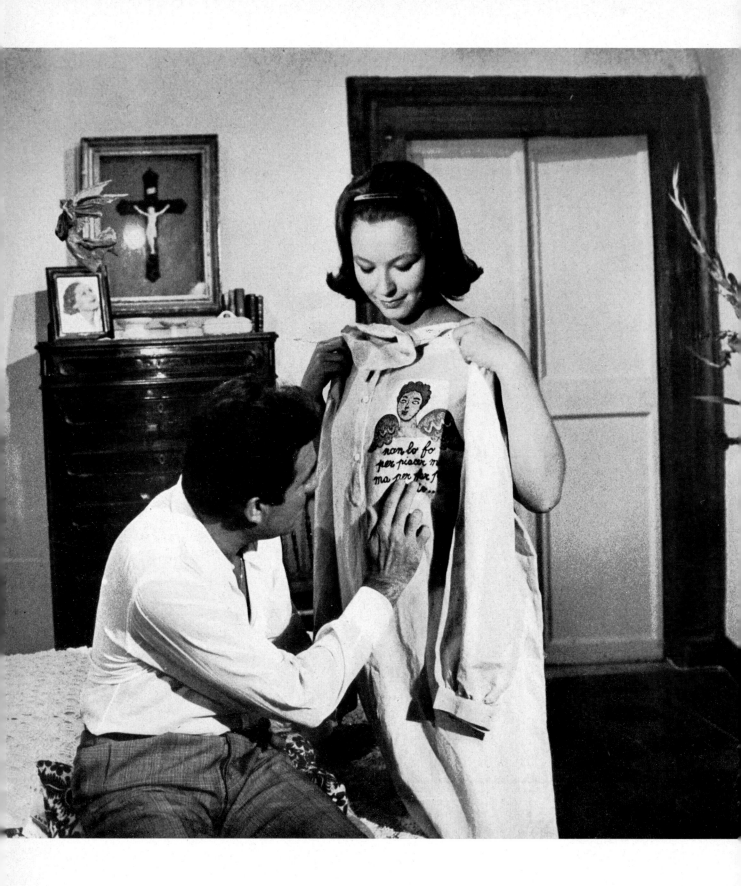

Marco Ferreri

L'APE REGINA - THE CONIUGAL BED

Ugo Tognazzi, Marina Vlady, Walter
Giller, Riccardo Fellini, Igi Polidoro,
Nino Vingelli, Jaqueline Perrier, Linda
Sini (Sancro Film - Les Films Marceau -
Cocinor, 1963).

Ferreri introduces macabre Anglo-Saxon humor into the Italian cinema — in Latin dress of course. But from the grotesque rhythms of The
Conjugal Bed, he is not always able to draw the ironical effects he
intends with the necessary levity.

FR3. Le lit conjugal. Dif. le 11.5.77.
Ugo TOGNAZZI. Marina VLADY.

MARINA VLADY   UGO TOGNAZZI

With **Sentimental Experiment**, after their contribution to the best Italian cinema as scriptwriters, Massimo Franciosa and Pasquale Festa Campanile start their directing career as intellectuals. But they give us characters at times remarkably well-drawn.

Pasquale Festa Campanile - Massimo Franciosa

UN TENTATIVO SENTIMENTALE
SENTIMENTAL EXPERIMENT

François Prévost, Jean Marc Bory, Leticia Roman, Barbara Steele, Gabriele Ferzetti, Giulio Bosetti (Franca Film, France Cinéma Production, 1964).

Ugo Gregoretti

I NUOVI ANGELI - THE NEW ANGELS

Nonprofessional actors (Arco Film, 1961).

OMICRON

Renato Salvatori, Rosemary Dexter (Lux - Ultra - Vides, 1963).

The language of the television inquiry is introduced into Italian cinema in Gregoretti's The New Angels; but it at once acquires the traditional rhythm of the cinema, although with quite a new type of humor, in Omicron, the first Italian science-fiction film.

227

Gualtiero Jacopetti
MONDO CANE

Nonprofessional actors (Cineriz, 1961).

Jacopetti photographs the world in his own way, showing up its strangest or worst aspects, those, at any rate, which can shock (Mondo Cane, Women of the World). He introduces a new genre into the cinema, but does not always base it on respect for truth. Indeed, his more sensational sequences often give the impression of being hoaxes. And while they are most effective as spectacle, they do not succeed in convincing with equal force as reasoned evidence.

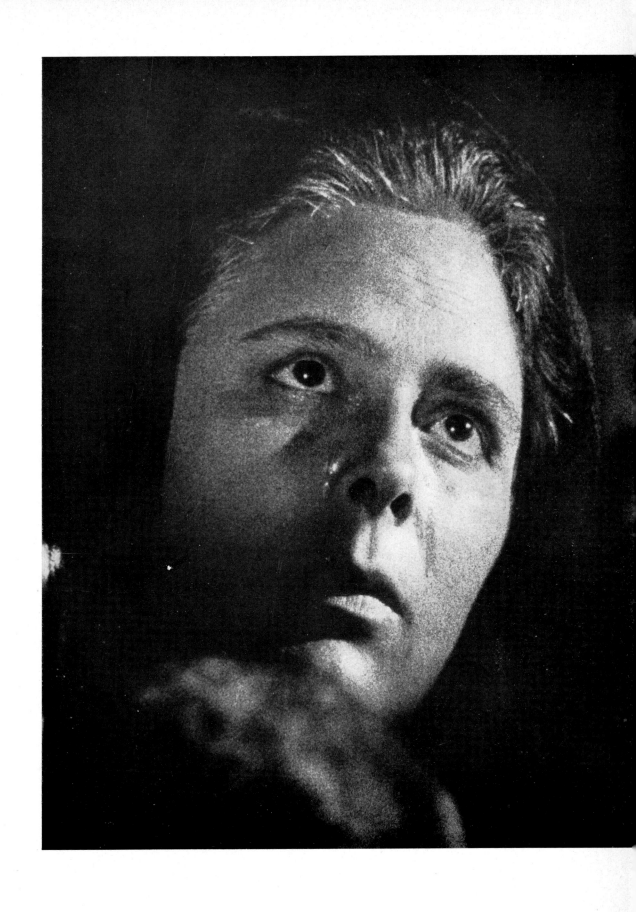

Gualtiero Jacopetti
LA DONNA NEL MONDO - WOMEN OF THE WORLD
Nonprofessional actors (Cineriz, 1962).

Nanni Loy

Un giorno da leoni
A day for lion-hearts

Renato Salvatori, Tomas Milian, Nino Castelnuovo, Romolo Valli, Saro Urzì, Corrado Pani, Franco Bucceri, Bruno Scipioni, Anna Maria Ferrero, Carla Gravina (Lux - Vides - Galatea, 1961).

For Nanni Loy, war memories are the best and most fertile inspiration for making films; he works with a language that never falters in A Day for Lion-Hearts.

Nanni Loy

LE QUATTRO GIORNATE DI NAPOLI
THE FOUR DAYS OF NAPLES

Nonprofessional actors (Titanus, 1963).

But his most successful attempt is The Four Days of Naples, a lyrical reconstruction, half-way between epic and melodrama, of the revolt at Naples in September 1943. It is produced with a realism which, while showing he had faithfully learned the severe lesson of neorealism, was expressed in a thoroughly fresh linguistic atmosphere, but always within the limits of a faithful historical reconstruction, both of the setting and the psychology.

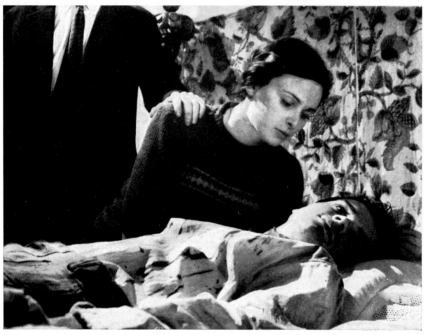

Francesco Maselli

GLI SBANDATI - THE STRAGGLERS

Lucia Bosè, Jean Pierre Mooky, Antonio De Teffè, Leonardo Botta, Evy Nicholson, Marco Guglielmi, Giuliano Montaldo, Goliarda Sapienza, Isa Miranda (C.V.C., 1955).

Maselli's directing always shows a rigorous formal perfection even when it is not supported by convincingly constructed stories. This is amply shown by The Dolphins, where, in spite of the lack of balance in the story and the characters, the detailed realization of the setting (even better than in The Stragglers) achieves the firm definition of a real and particular character; and this is perhaps the most important thing.

Francesco Maselli

I DELFINI - THE DOLPHINS

Claudia Cardinale, Gérard Blain, Anna Maria Ferrero, Betsy Blair, Antonella Lualdi, Tomas Milian, Sergio Fantoni, Claudio Gora (Lux - Vides, 1960).

With Gli Indifferenti, based on Moravia's novel, Maselli exposes people who, in their desolate cynism, are no less vivid and impressive than those described in the literary work itself.

Francesco Maselli
GLI INDIFFERENTI
Claudia Cardinale, Shelley Winters, Paulette Goddard, Rod Steiger, Tomas Milian (Lux-Vetro-Vides, 1963).

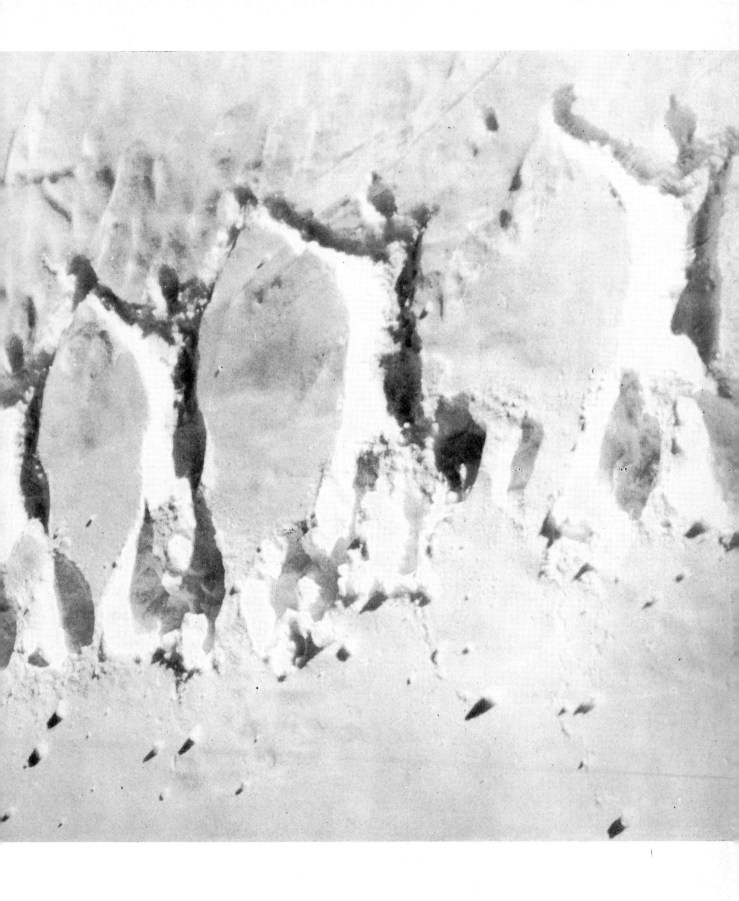

Olmi's style is simple, quiet, deliberately subdued. In his first film, Time Has Stopped, he already displays high formal qualities, allied to a very keen psychological insight.

Ermanno Olmi

IL TEMPO SI È FERMATO - TIME HAS STOPPED

Natale Rossi, Paolo Quadrubbi (Lux Film, 1959).

239

Ermanno Olmi

IL POSTO - THE SOUND OF TRUMPETS

Loredana Detto, Sandro Panzeri (Titanus - The 24 Horses, 1961).

Olmi's style is even more mature in The Sound of Trumpets, a slice
of middle-class life described with a minuteness of realistic detail and,
at the same time, with an almost ethereal poetic truth. This work
exhibits a perfect narrative balance and a sure psychological understanding. All merits in The Fiancés are a little marred by a certain
esoteric fad of the intellectual cinema, which leads even some directors of serious standing to take insufficient trouble over the spectacle
aspect.

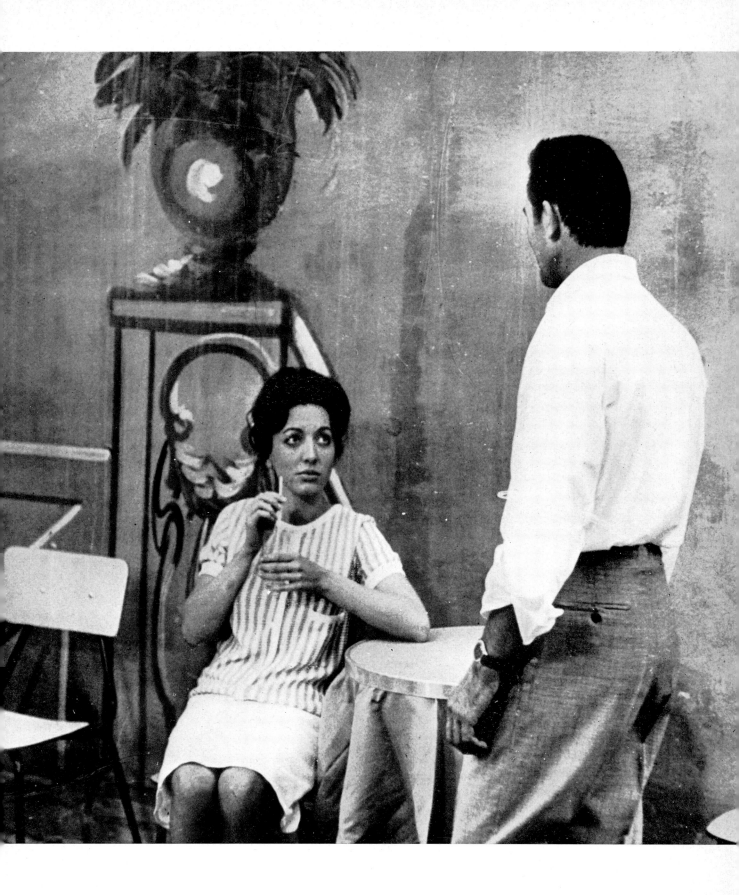

Ermanno Olmi

I FIDANZATI - THE FIANCES

Carlo Cabrini, Anna Canzi (Titanus Sicilia - Soc. Edit. Cinemat., It. 22 dicembre, 1963).

Valentino Orsini, Paolo Taviani, Vittorio Taviani

UN UOMO DA BRUCIARE - A MAN TO BURN

Gian Maria Volonté, Didi Perego, Spyro, Fokas, Lidia Alfonsi, Marina Malfatti, Vittorio Duse, Sandro Sperlì, Turi Ferro (Ager Film - Sancro Film - Alfa Cinematografica, 1962).

The merit of A Man to Burn lies above all in the psychological portrayal of the protagonist, deliberately held poised between contradictions and opposing sentiments: a character who, in spite of the lack of balance in the text which he dominates, often attains credibility.

Pier Paolo Pasolini

ACCATTONE - THE BEGGAR

Franco Citti, Franca Pasut, Silvana Corsini, Paola Guidi, Adriana Asti, Mario Cipriani (Arco Film - Cino Del Duca, 1961).

The encounter between painting and reality, discovered by Visconti in The Earth Trembles, is rediscovered anew in our days by Pasolini. His The Beggar, however, is not only an interchange, often insufficiently matured, between the cinema and the plastic arts, but is also literature streaked with realism and sentimentality. The photography often follows in the wake of Buñuel's more intellectual and baroque works.

Film Forum

Anna Magnani, as the title character singing at her former pimp's wedding in "Mamma Roma."

FILM REVIEW

A Steamy Pasolini Rarity From 1962

Hell hath no fury like Mamma Roma, the virago played so stormily by Anna Magnani in Pier Paolo Pasolini's astonishing 1962 film. Along with its obvious echoes of Italian postwar neo-realism, including explicit references to works by Roberto Rossellini and Vittorio De Sica, the previously obscure "Mamma Roma" also seethes with the sensuality and dark iconoclasm that would mark Pasolini's subsequent career.

Indeed, beyond this film's stark visual beauty and its madly inappropriate Biblical references, there lies a murky, overheated sexual melodrama suggestive of Tennessee Williams, himself a great admirer of La Magnani's raw histrionic style. Here she plays a former prostitute who brings a feverish, unexamined intensity to the job of bringing up her sexually ripe adolescent son. The boy's destiny is thus shaped in fearsome ways by his mother's eroticism. Mamma Jocasta would have been more like it.

"Mamma Roma," which opens today at the Film Forum, is a fascinating rarity, a film not even presented at museum screenings in America until 1990. It was the second feature (after "Accattone") made by this protean and increasingly perverse film maker, poet, novelist and playwright, whose later, more feverish works included "The Decameron," "The Canterbury Tales" and "The Arabian Nights."

By the time of his murder in 1975, Pasolini's vision had reached the sordid excesses of "Salo," which has in recent months been the basis for an obscenity case against a Cincinnati video store that made the film available for rental. It was a long way to that film's scatological extremes from the relative restraint of "Mamma Roma."

Still under the influence of his neorealist forbears, Pasolini conceived a central character resembling Ms. Magnani's Pina, the heroine of Rossellini's "Open City," who dies while pregnant at the end of that 1945 landmark but is essentially revived in 1962 as the mother of a teen-age son. Though her eruptive acting style is slightly tamed by Pasolini's meticulous, deliberate direction, Ms. Magnani has lost none of her witchy gusto in this role.

Mamma Roma is first seen delivering taunts at a country wedding, which Pasolini staged to resemble the Last Supper even though the bride is faintly grotesque and the groom is Carmine (Franco Citti), Mamma Roma's former pimp. With typical restraint, Mamma Roma makes this first appearance shepherding pigs in hats and mocking Italy's national anthem. The elegance of this film's beautiful black-and-white cinematography (by Tonino Delli Colli) is never matched by any corresponding delicacy to its drama.

"You laugh like a pair of bellows," one man at the wedding tells Mamma Roma, and it's true. She greets each development in this tempestuous story with a robust, mocking vitality that the film celebrates with-

Anna Magnani, of course, isn't your ordinary mom.

son in an ecstatic, prurient tango, "Mamma Roma" revels in the endless lurid nuances of its story. That they happen to contrast mightily with Pasolini's images of Mamma Roma and Ettore as Madonna and Christ is only one small part of this film's eccentricity. Shot either in velvety nighttime, where Mamma Roma is the queen of casual Roman decadence, or in sun-baked, midday landscapes that create an effortlessly torrid atmosphere, the story imprisons its characters in a world of temptation.

Ettore falls under the spell of a compliant young woman named Bruna, who can be had for the price of cheap jewelry and who also happily accommodates all the other young men Ettore has become friends with. The camera's meaningful appraisals of these sultry young men become part of the film's insinuating manner. Meanwhile, when the mother learns what her son has been up

made a boy!" and then persuades a prostitute to lure him away from Bruna. In this atmosphere, it's indeed hard for Pasolini to shape "Mamma Roma" as a story of righteousness and the hope for redemption. But he tries.

tainly in order once Mamma Roma resumes contact with Ettore (Ettore Garofolo), the son she had abandoned and now chooses to guide toward respectability. Liberated from prostitution in fact if not in mannerisms, Mamma Roma now plans to sell produce in the marketplace and make a good life for her son. From their first moments in Rome together, with mother leading son.

"Have you seen the Devil, or what?" someone asks Mamma Roma during the story. With her pitch-black hair, haggard eyes and bottomless well of emotion, Ms. Magnani suggests that she has seen things her audience can barely imagine, and that she struggles against her own memories every day. In a couple of the film's remarkably stylized sequences, she strolls through the streets of Rome by night and recites the story of her life to whoever walks beside her, as if "Mamma Roma" were on the verge of becoming a work of musical theater. Pasolini's score for the film, incidentally, relies heavily on Vivaldi for the rich sense of forboding this story needs.

Beyond the excitingly overwrought Magnani, the film's cast consists mostly of voluptuous-looking nonprofessionals with the appropriately sinister air. (Mr. Citti, whose brother Sergio collaborated with Pasolini on the screenplay, spent time in jail while filming was under way.) Minor characters in the credits are variously listed as "thug," "pimp," "male prostitute" and so on. One familiar face is that of Lamberto Maggiorani, so stirringly memorable as the father in "The Bicycle Thief," who here plays a hospital patient robbed by Ettore as Mamma Roma's hopes for him prove futile. Only a film maker of Pasolini's dauntlessly operatic intensity could follow the boy's petty crime with imagery suggesting the Crucifixion.

In Mamma Roma, Pasolini repeats the same aesthetic attitudes we had in The Beggar, poorly supported this time by a story leaning too easily towards popular sentimentality, although it has some very effective dramatic close-ups.

Pier Paolo Pasolini

MAMMA ROMA

Anna Magnani, Ettore Garofolo, Franco Citti, Silvana Corsini, Luisa Loiano, Paolo Volponi, Luciano Gonini, Vittorio La Paglia, Piero Morgia (Arco Film - Cineriz, 1962).

Although uneven in its dramatic intensity, The Gospel According to Matthew shows that Pasolini has generally succeeded in adapting the Sacred Text to the cinematic art.

Pier Paolo Pasolini

IL VANGELO SECONDO MATTEO
THE GOSPEL ACCORDING TO MATTEW

Enrique, Irazoqui, Margherita Caruso, Susanna Pasolini, Marcello Norante, Mario Socrate (Arco Film-Lux, 1964).

249

Vito Pandolfi

GLI ULTIMI - THE LAST

Adolfo Galli and nonprofessional actors (Le Grazie Film, 1963).

In Vito Pandolfi's The Last, we have strict attention to form and images of consummate beauty. But the story does not yet know how to conform to the requirements of cinema narrative, and indulges too freely in pauses and static patches.

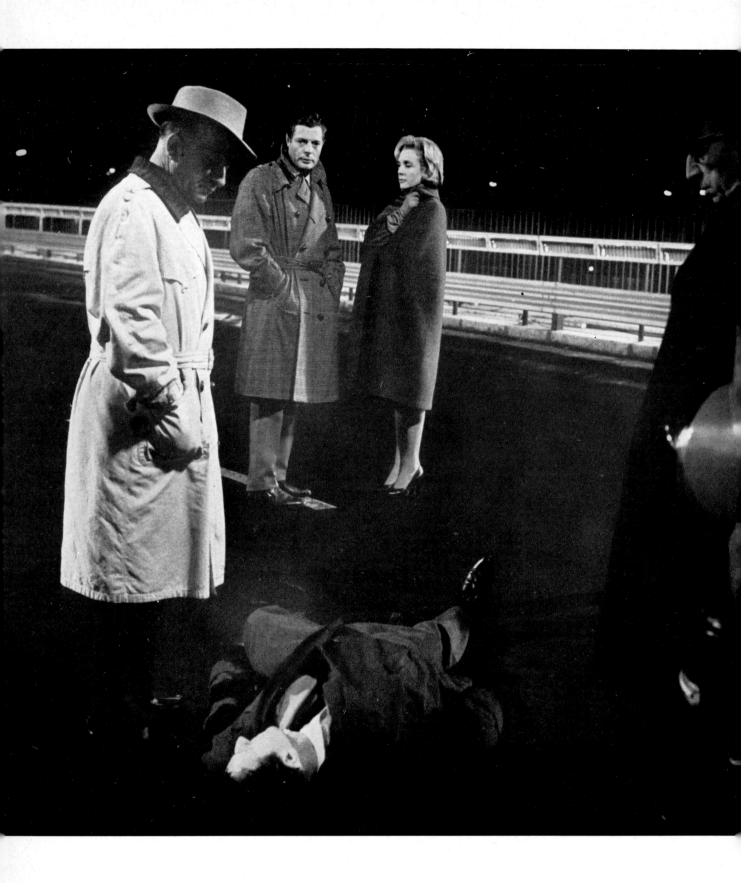

Elio Petri

L'assassino - The murder

Marcello Mastroianni, Micheline Presle,
Cristina Gajoni, Salvo Randone, Enrico
Maria Salerno, Corrado Zingaro, Paolo
Panelli (Titanus - Vides, 1961).

After a first film carefully constructed from the point of view of the intelligent spectacle (The Murder) and a work of taut stylistic rigor (The Days Are Numbered), Petri tackles literature in The Schoolteacher from Vigevano. Here he displays a rich visual understanding, but does not achieve altogether convincing results because of the harshness of a text, more than anything else, in which the psychology is left with too many loose ends.

Elio Petri

IL MAESTRO DI VIGEVANO
THE SCHOOLTEACHER FROM VIGEVANO
Alberto Sordi, Claire Bloom (De Laurentiis Cinemat. S.p.A., 1963).

Gillo Pontecorvo

Kapo'

Susan Strasberg, Laurent Terzieff, Emmanuelle Riva, Didi Perego, Gianni Garko, Annabella Besi, Graziella Galvani (Vides - Zebra Film - Cineriz, 1960).

Superb realistic photography and harsh drama impeccably stated and worked out from the psychological point of view — this is Gillo Pontecorvo's Kapò, a film that reveals genuine talent.

Folco Quilici

L'ULTIMO PARADISO - LAST PARADISE

Nonprofessional actors (Paneuropa, 1956).

Folco Quilici's explorations are always something more than a travel journal. They are reportage of states of mind as well as of surroundings, couched in a narrative vein which is rarely concerned only with external factors.

Folco Quilici

TI-KOYO E IL SUO PESCECANE
TI-KOYO AND HIS SHARK

Marlene Among, Al Kauwe, Denis Pouï-
ra, Diane Samsoi, Roau (Titanus - Metro - S.N.P.C. - S.G.C., 1962).

This manner of Quilici's is seen above all in Ti-Koyo and His Shark.
It is a documentary report on the South Seas, but a story is grafted
onto it which has all the appearance of truth. And the two aspects,
which you would expect to be at variance, always manage to remain in
limpid, graceful balance.

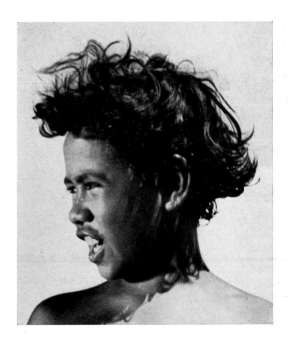

Very hard sequences, inwardly driven by clear dramatic force but not always integrated with the narrative; an ethnographical reconstruction of the personal agony of one man — this is Brunello Rondi's Il Demonio.

Brunello Rondi

IL DEMONIO

Daliah Lavi, Giovanni Cristofanelli, Nicola Tagliacozzo, Frank Wolf (Titanus - Vox Film - Les Films Marceau - Cocinor, 1963).

Luciano Salce

Il federale - The federal

Ugo Tognazzi, George Wilson, Stefania
Sandrelli, Mirelle Granelli, Elsa Vazzoler, Renzo Palmer, Gianni Agus, Gianrico Tedeschi (Dino De Laurentiis S.p.A.
1961).

**Into the comedy of contemporary manners, Luciano Salce brings a
shadow, often a clever shadow, of intellectual indignation, especially
evident in certain passages of that ironical sketch, The Federal.**

Luciano Salce

LA VOGLIA MATTA - CRAZY DESIRE

Ugo Tognazzi, Catherine Spaak, Gianni
Garko, Beatrice Altariba, Jimmy Fontana, Franco Giacobini, Fabrizio Cappucci, Margherita Girelli, Oliviero Prunas, Stelvio Rosi, Lylia Neyung (Dino
De Laurentiis S.p.A., 1962).

The same irony, but supported by serious aims at psychological insight, is found in Crazy Desire, a delightful portrait of a forty-year-old at loggerheads with teen-agers.

EHEN ZU DRITT

ELITE-FILM zeigt:

„EHEN ZU DRITT"

(Alta infedelta)

mit Charles Aznavour, Bernard Blier, Claire Bloom, Jean-Pierre Cassel, Nino Manfredi, Michele Mercier, Ugo Tognazzi, Monica Vitti

Regie: Mario Monicelli, Elio Petri, Franco Rossi, Luciano Salce
Buch: Age Scarpelli, Scola Maccari

Francesco	Nino Manfredi
Raffaella	Fulvia Franco
Ronald	John Law

Regie: Franco Rossi — Kamera: Ennio Guarnieri

Die langjährige Ehe zwischen Raffaella und dem braven, wenn auch ein bißchen trägen Francesco ist auf ein totes Gleis geraten. Nicht zuletzt deshalb nützt Raffaella die Gelegenheit eines Ferienaufenthaltes in einem Badeort, etwas zu flirten. Eigentlich nur, um ihren Mann ein wenig eifersüchtig zu machen. Besonders ausdauernd widmet sich ihr ein blutjunger blonder Engländer.
Francesco wird das schließlich zu bunt, und er stellt den Playboy heftig zur Rede. Dieser erklärt fassungslos, daß er sich überhaupt nicht für Frauen interessiere, sondern . . . und ein vielsagender Blick trifft den großen, stattlichen Francesco . . . Raffaella kann es sich überhaupt nicht erklären, warum ihr Mann hemmungslos lacht, als sie darauf besteht, den Urlaub vorzeitig abzubrechen. Offenbar kommt Francesco überhaupt nicht auf den Gedanken, wie tapfer sie der Verführung widerstanden hat. Weil sie eben eine anständige Frau ist . . .

Giulo	Charles Aznavour
Laura	Claire Bloom

Regie: Elio Petri — Kamera: Ennio Guarnieri

Er ist ein eleganter, etwas melancholischer Mann — Sie eine faszinierende, mondäne Frau. Beide haben so ungefähr das gleiche persönliche Schicksal. Seit sieben Jahren verheiratet, stehen ihre Ehen nur noch auf dem Papier. Kein Wunder, daß sich die beiden Enttäuschten im Gleichklang ihrer Seelen rasch näherkommen und schließlich sogar eine Liebesstunde verbringen. Wobei er, Giulio, offenbar das Gefühl hat, diese etwas rätselhafte Frau schon zu kennen. Oder spielt er nur mit in einem absonderlichen Spiel? Am Abend kehrt er nach Hause zurück. Er will sich mit seiner Frau gründlich aussprechen, die — wie sie ihm offen gesteht — auch an diesem Nachmittag untreu war . . .
Eine seltsame Liebesverwirrung kommt zutage.

Gloria	. . . .	Monica Vitti
Tonio	. . . .	Jean-Pierre Cassel
Paolo	. . . .	Sergio Fantoni

Regie: Luciane Salce — Kamera: Ennio Guarnieri
Produktion: Gianni Hecht Lucari. Documento Film

Paolo ist mit der bildhübschen, reizvollen Gloria verheiratet. Nur leider ist sie geradezu irrsinnig eifersüchtig. Von früh bis spät macht sie ihm Szenen und verdächtigt alle Frauen der Welt, ihren Mann zu becircen — mit seiner Einwilligung natürlich. Immer wieder gibt es Krach. Paolo hat das eines Tages satt und rennt davon, um sich, wie er hinterläßt, für immer von ihr zu trennen. Jetzt läuft Gloria zu großer Form auf. Mit bitteren Tränen beklagt sie sich bei Paolos Freund Tonino und erklärt ihm mit soviel Verve, sich umbringen zu wollen, daß dieser all seinen Charme aufwendet, um die unglückliche Ehefrau zu trösten. Wie weit ist er dabei gegangen? Ob man es jemals erfahren wird? Zwar ist Gloria eifrig dabei, ihrer Freundin die Sache am Telefon ganz genau zu erklären — aber leider wird das Gespräch unterbrochen. . .

Cesare	. . . .	Ugo Tognazzi
Tebaide	. . . .	Michele Mercier
Reguzzoni	. . . .	Bernard Blier

Regie: Mario Monicelli — Kamera: Gianni di Venanzo

Der Fabrikant Cesare Bertolazzi ist ein fleißiger Mann und biederer Familienvater. Nur leider packt ihn von Zeit zu Zeit der Spielteufel, und dann vergißt er alles. Sogar seine guten Vorsätze.
So kommt es, daß er bei riskantem Spiel alles verliert, Haus, Lieferwagen und sogar seine Fabrik. Da macht ihm sein Gläubiger Reguzzoni einen unglaublichen Vorschlag: er ist bereit, die gesamte Schuld zu löschen, gegen eine einzige Liebesnacht mit Bertolazzis schöner Frau Tebaide. Natürlich weist Cesare diese Zumutung empört zurück, dann aber beginnt er zu überlegen — und schließlich hilft ihm Tebaide selbst, indem sie mit weiblichem Raffinement den liebestrunkenen Reguzzoni um den geforderten Preis prellt. Dennoch entsteht tiefes Mißtrauen zwischen Cesare und seiner Frau, bis Cesare wutentbrannt zum Jagdgewehr greift und seinem Nebenbuhler einen Denkzettel verabreicht. Und nun muß der nichtbetrogene Ehemann in der Öffentlichkeit den Gehörnten spielen — denn nur dann wird das Gericht ihm mildernde Umstände wegen berechtigter Eifersucht zubilligen.

Eigentümer: Leminger, Spalding und Weiss. Für den Inhalt verantwortlich: R. Leminger, Wien VII,
Lindengasse 43, Tel. 93 64 53. Alleinherstellungsrecht für Österreich. Nachdruck (auch auszugsweise)
nur mit Erlaubnis gestattet. Druck: Gröpner O.H.G., Wien VII, Kirchengasse 34
Abonnement: 40 Nummern zu S 30,— (ca. 12mal jährlich).

Luciano Salce

LA CUCCAGNA - A STROKE OF LUCK

Donatella Turri, Luigi Tenco, Umberto D'Orsi (C.I.R.A.C. - Giorgio Agliani Cinematografica, 1962).

LE ORE DELL'AMORE - HOURS OF LOVE

Ugo Tognazzi, Emanuelle Riva, Barbara Steele, Umberto D'Orsi, Mara Berni, (Dino De Laurentiis S.p.A., 1963).

Vancini's photography confirms the talents he showed in documentary films, where he was especially careful to transform settings and background into characters. In The Long Night of '43, however, the real characters do not stand out so well. The more dramatic states of mind only spring, for the most part, from the surroundings or from the chorus.

Florestano Vancini

La lunga notte del '43
The long night of '43

Belinda Lee, Gabriele Ferzetti, Enrico Maria Salerno, Andrea Checchi, Nerio Bernard, Gino Cervi, (Ajace Film - Euro International Film, 1960).

Florestano Vancini
LA BANDA CASAROLI - THE CASAROLI GANG
Renato Salvatori, Jean Claude Brialy, Calisti, Gabriella Zanetti, Marcella Rovena, Isa Quario, Marcello Tusco, Michele Sakara, Adriano Micantoni (Documento Film, 1962).

LA CALDA VITA
Catherine Spaak, Gabriele Ferzetti, Jacques Perrin, Fabrizio Capucci (Jolly Film, 1963).

The characters of The Casaroli Gang are more mature, but their agony, although drawn very clearly from the psychological point of view, is not always supported by a straightforward story.

Eriprando Visconti

UNA STORIA MILANESE - A STORY IN MILAN

Daniéle Gaubert, Enrico Thibaut, Romolo Valli, Lucilla Morlacchi, Regina Bianchi, Giancarlo Dettori, Rosanna Armani, Ermanno Olmi (Galatea, 1962).

Lina Wertmüller's The Basilisks is another melancholy ode in the Italian provincial style, successful above all in evoking a group state of mind and in accurately depicting a locale.

Lina Wertmüller

I BASILISCHI - THE BASILISKS

Toni Petruzzi, Stefano Sattoflores, Sergio Ferrannino, Enzo Di Vecchio, Marisa Omodei, Manlio Blais, Luigi Barbieri, Flora Carabella, Mimmina Quirico, Rosetta Palumbo, Rosanna Santoro (22 Dicembre - Galatea, 1963).

INDEXES

INDEX

Actors and directors

STATEN ISLAND INSTITUTE OF ARTS AND SCIENCES

Staten Island Museum • High Rock Park Conservation Center • William T. Davis Wildlife Refuge

FILM SERIES '89
MICHELANGELO ANTONIONI

JANUARY

8 Sunday, 1:30 pm
Nettezza Urbana, 1948, 9 minutes
L'Avventura, 1960, 145 minutes

15 Sunday, 1:30 pm
La Notte, 1961, 122 minutes, with commentator Bruce Elder

22 Sunday, 1:30 pm
L'Eclisse, 1962, 124 minutes, with commentator P. Adams Sitney

29 Sunday, 1:30 pm
Cronaca di un Amore, 1950, 96 minutes
Tentato Suicidio, 1953, 20 minutes

FEBRUARY

5 Sunday, 1:30 pm
La Signora Senza Camelie, 1953, 105 minutes

12 Sunday, 1:30 pm
Nettezza Urbana, 1948, 9 minutes. *Deserto Rosso*, 1964, 116 minutes, with commentator Giuliana Bruno

16 Thursday, 7:00 pm
[This program at Anthology Film Archives in Manhattan, at 32-34 Second Avenue.]
Gente Del Po, 1947, 10 minutes

L'Amorosa Menzogna, 1949, 10 minutes

Superstizione, 1949, 9 minutes

Le Amiche, 1955, 104 minutes

19 Sunday, 1:30 pm
Blow Up, 1966, 111 minutes

26 Sunday, 1:30 pm
Zabriskie Point, 1970, 110 minutes, with commentator Robert Haller

MARCH

5 Sunday, 1:30 pm
To be announced.

All films at the Museum of the Staten Island Institute unless otherwise noted. These screenings and the gallery exhibition are supported by the New York State Council on the Arts, Film/Video Arts, the Department of Cultural Affairs of the City of New York, the Italian Cultural Institute, and Island Cinema Resources of Staten Island. We are also indebted to the Cineteca Nazionale in Rome, the Museum of Modern Art in New York, and Pacific Film Archives in Berkely for the loan of films, photographs, and services for these projects.

The Staten Island Institute of Arts and Sciences is Staten Island's oldest cultural institution and administers the Staten Island Museum, the Library and Archives, High Rock Park Conservation Center, the William T. Davis Wildlife Refuge, Evergreen Park, and Reeds Basket Willow Swamp. The Institute is supported in part by the City of New York through an annual appropriation from the Department of Cultural Affairs.□

MICHELANGELO ANTONIONI:
THE ENCHANTED MOUNTAINS

Michelangelo Antonioni has been making paintings—abstract and representational—for at least as long as he has been making films. But because he has never allowed them to be seen by the public, or even by many friends, the very existence of this work by one of our greatest film-makers has been unknown. This exhibition, *The Enchanted Mountains*, is the first American show of Antonioni's paintings. The origin of *The Enchanted Mountains* was a series of color tests Antonioni made before shooting began on his first color film, *The Red Desert (Deserto Rosso)* in 1964. By mixing tempera and oil paints on different paper surfaces, Antonioni made the colors that were used in the film, including the painting of whole streets and trees. Six years then passed before he returned to this particular medium (during this time he made both *Blow Up*, 1965, and *Zabriskie Point*, 1970).Starting in the early 1970s, and continuing up through 1985, Antonioni made more than 180 prints in *The Enchanted Mountains* series. In each case he mixed colors on several different paper surfaces, but also had these works collaged, photographed, enlarged and color filtered. The product of this process, which Antonioni performs directly, or supervises in the darkroom, is this photographic series.In 1980 some friends urged him to show the prints to the public, but Antonioni demurred. For two more years he refused these requests, but finally agreed in 1983; their first public exposure came at the Galleria Nazionale d'Arte Moderna from 8 October to 27 November, in conjunction with the Venice Film Festival's award to Antonioni of its Golden Lion for his career in film. Antonioni chose not to comment on the meaning of these works in the catalog for that 1983 show in Rome, save for the title, "Le montagne incantate." In that catalog he limits himself to some basic notes that the photographic enlargement process, like that in the film *Blow Up*, makes visible details "invisible in the original" collage paintings. However, his title *The Enchanted Mountains* suggests a great deal about the pictures; many can easily be perceived as landscapes. But if some are analogous to mountain ranges, others appear to be almost microscopic details of

glacial formations, or aerial perspectives of eroded terrain. These latter readings then prompt us to revise our sense of the "mountain" images. Their depth becomes uncertain, as well as such factors as orientation in space; the juxtaposition of textures and the identification of "horizons" are additional variables. This shifting, this transformation of what we see into what we can not know, contributes to the "enchantment" of the series. The pictures also suggest, in some cases, surrealist frottage, Japanese landscapes, and the luminous paintings of J.M.W. Turner. Of all the comparisons we can seek, the most obvious and most difficult is to Antonioni's films. Visually there are few parallels, but in metaphoric terms the divergent forces of older and more recent moralities, of male disconnection with emotions and honesty, and the female integration of them, are mirrored in these pictures where earth meets air, or less specifically, where one form of matter encounters another.

Robert Haller
Curator of Film, Staten Island
Institute of Arts and Sciences

Film Titles

Producers

ERRATA

Page	19	for	Nando Buzzanca	read	Lando Buzzanca
»	36	»	For Truths	»	Four Truths
»	42	»	Rick Bataglia	»	Rick Battaglia
»	89	»	Giulia Rubino	»	Giulia Rubini
»	98	»	Antony Quinn	»	Anthony Quinn
»	129	»	Norma Bengell	»	Norma Benguell
»	132	»	Acktung Banditi	»	Achtung Banditi
»	156	»	Window	»	Widower
»	161	»	Dialine	»	Dialina
»	188	»	ycelds	»	yields
»	195	»	William	»	Williams
»	190	»	withim	»	within
»	212	»	the beggars	»	the beggar
»	234	»	Jean Pierre Mooky	»	Jean Pierre Mocky
»	269	»	Isa Quario	»	Isa Querio